ITALIAN COASTAL

To my loves, Matthew and Milo, with whom I could
happily travel these or any seas forever

RECIPES AND STORIES FROM
WHERE THE LAND MEETS THE SEA

ITALIAN COASTAL

AMBER GUINNESS

PHOTOGRAPHY BY SAGHAR SETAREH

CONTENTS

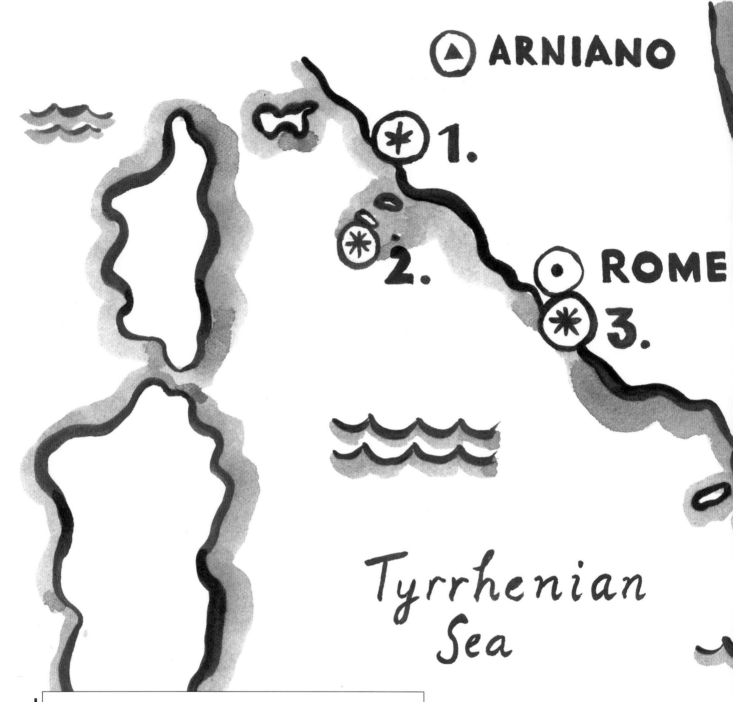

ARNIANO

ROME

1.

2.

3.

Tyrrhenian
Sea

7.

INTRODUCTION

It was as I bobbed in the crystal-clear waters off Punta Scario beach on the island of Salina that I truly began to appreciate the magical and restorative powers of the Tyrrhenian Sea. It had been a tough few months – I was juggling three jobs at the time and felt like I was being pulled in a million directions – but as I swam out towards the island of Vulcano, a cartoonishly conical active volcano, I felt all my worries drain away. Yes, I was on holiday, so of course my mood was bound to lift, but as I floated there, gazing back at the beach with its mounds of softly polished black pebbles, I realised that so many of my favourite spots in Italy have something in common: they are all scattered across this particular body of water.

The Tyrrhenian laps against Italy's west coast. It comprises a large expanse of sea enclosed by the Tuscan archipelago in the north, mainland Italy's western coast to the east, Sardinia and Corsica to the west, and Sicily to the south. The intense contentment I felt on that salty sunny day reminded me of scorching hot summers when I was young, on the ferry with my parents to the island of Giglio – a three-hour door-to-door trip from my childhood home, Arniano, in Tuscany – excitedly anticipating plunging into the cool waters. And years later, on holiday with my husband, splashing on the stony beach of Marina del Cantone near Naples.

I was brought up in southern Tuscany, so have always lived close to the Tyrrhenian. When my sister and I were little, as a family we would explore miles of Tuscany's coastline. A visit to La Maremma, Tuscany's southern coastal area, with its sandy beaches at Ansedonia, Macchiatonda and L'Ultima Spiaggia, was only an hour and a half's drive away. My parents would often bundle us into the car for a Sunday excursion to visit friends who spent their summers by the beach, where we would spend the day swimming, making sandcastles and feasting on bowls of spaghetti alle vongole. On days when we were feeling more energetic we would take the hour-long ferry crossing to the island of Giglio, enjoying the simple beauty of the pastel-coloured port town. But as I grew older I realised that these were only a few of the gems dotted across the Tyrrhenian Sea.

To say the names of the Tyrrhenian's better-known islands and mainland destinations is like playing a word association game where the answers would be 'La Dolce Vita' and 'delicious food': Naples, the Amalfi Coast, Capri, Sorrento and Ischia in Campania; the Aeolian Islands off Sicily's northern coast; and Palermo to the west. These glamorous-sounding places always seemed far away and, while we knew the Tuscan coast well, my childhood only afforded me a limited knowledge of other parts of the Tyrrhenian.

One exception happened during an ill-fated holiday in 1997, the year of the Macarena dance craze, when my uncle and aunt rented a villa on the north-eastern coast of Sicily. My parents, sister and I caught the overnight ferry from Naples to Messina, but because it was August the ferry was packed and we had to find a patch of floor to sleep on. When we arrived everyone was excited to be reunited with our extended family, but unfortunately the mood didn't last long as the island was hit by the worst storm in years, leading to major flooding. The children outnumbered the adults by three to one so spare a thought for our poor parents while we were all stuck inside, watching cars being washed down the street. Even when the rain abated, the mounds of mud were incredible. Looking back, that visit was an early indicator of the sometimes violent nature of this seemingly Arcadian land.

The Tyrrhenian was named by the Greeks after the seafaring Etruscans who inhabited the Tuscan coast (Tyrrhenian is Greek for 'Etruscan'). The name has always made me feel close to this body of water as the house where I grew up (Arniano) is surrounded by old Etruscan settlements. Our local hilltop village of Murlo even has an Etruscan museum, though nothing actually useful like a tabacchi or bar. The Tyrrhenian is also the sea of *The Odyssey*, with much of Homer's epic purported to have taken place in its waters. Monte Circeo in Lazio is supposed to be Aeaea, the nymph Circe's enchanted island where Odysseus's men were turned into swine. Punta Campanella, the Amalfi Coast's most westerly point, is apparently where Odysseus escaped the siren's cursed song, and the Aeolian Islands off Sicily's northern coast are where he and his men rested after their exhausting encounter with the Cyclops. These myths underpin the magical feel of these already-enchanting places which capture one so viscerally with their natural beauty.

Aside from the myths and history of the Tyrrhenian, the local produce and culinary traditions have sharpened my interest in this area. With so much volcanic activity, the soil surrounding Vesuvius, Etna and Vulcano is rich with minerals, making the vegetables more bountiful and intense in flavour than those grown in other parts of the southern Mediterranean. People lucky enough to live in these places have come up with some glorious ways to cook their vegetables, often served with a simple grilled fish plucked from the sea that morning.

All the major destinations of the Tyrrhenian retain their own distinct style of cooking. In fact, what makes this region of the Mediterranean so remarkable is its culinary variety, despite being so closely linked by geography and sharing almost identical produce. Tuscany has a frugal yet hearty cuisine that brilliantly elevates the humblest ingredients without sacrificing flavour. Campania, the tomato-growing capital with Vesuvius at its heart, has a more fiery and playful palate. The Aeolian Islands, so remote and cut off from the rest of the world, have developed a cooking style that celebrates the produce of the islands: capers, oregano and lemons. And Sicily, conquered over millennia by every major civilisation, enjoys a kaleidoscopic blend of cuisines and influences: Italian food with an African, Greek, Arabic and Moorish twist.

This book is not intended to be an exhaustive investigation of the seven Italian regions that sit on the Tyrrhenian Sea. Whole volumes have been written about Sardinia and Calabria, two regions I am still eagerly getting to know. But for now, in this collection of recipes and stories, I hope to transport you to the shimmering waters of the Tyrrhenian via plates of pasta, baked fish and glasses of peach-laced white wine.

A NOTE ON THE RECIPES

 I have endeavoured to make this book as user-friendly as possible, indicating which recipes lend themselves to mass cooking, and which are better suited to just two or four people. To make a zucchini frittata for six, for example, would require three frying pans and is bound to send you into a tailspin, not to mention leaving a mountain of washing up. So the servings vary, simply because I like to make some dishes for small groups and others for larger ones. Equally, many of the recipes that appear to take ages can be broken into stages, or largely prepared the day before and then thrown together at the last minute. Zucchini lasagne, for instance, can be made ahead or even frozen, then simply popped in the oven when you're ready, banishing unnecessary stress when you have company. To help you plan I have included preparation and cooking times, and indicated where additional hands-off time is needed for cooling, chilling, setting and so on, so if you are on a tight schedule, you may want to skim read the recipe to factor these in.

The recipes from this part of Italy's western coast naturally veer from the absurdly simple, frugal and 'thrown together' to an intense kind of cooking typical of much cucina povera (poor cooking): slow and designed to bring out the best of simple ingredients. Please remember to always taste as you go; this is the key to preparing truly delicious food, and is the basis of all good cooking.

For consistency, oven temperatures are given in both Celsius and Fahrenheit for a fan-forced oven. If your oven is conventional, increase the temperature by about 20°C (70°F).

Some of the recipes in this book have been shared by some wonderful locals I met over the years and so I have tried to stay as true to the original as possible while also making them accessible to the home cook. This has meant that in some of the recipes, very specific quantities of parsley, pine nuts, onion, capers etc. are called for. But please do not be put off if you would prefer to take a looser approach. The recipes will work just fine whether you toss in a handful or a teaspoon.

PRODUCE AND INGREDIENTS FROM THE TYRRHENIAN

 The food of the Tyrrhenian is as varied as the places that make it special. The cuisine of the Maremma differs from that of the Amalfi Coast, just as food in Ponza differs from that in Sicily. There are great distances between these regions but they are united by the same sea, and by their climate and soils, so inevitably many of the same things grow all along Italy's western coast and its islands. An engrained philosophy of only championing what is available (and making do with what is to hand) means that throughout this book certain ingredients appear again and again. These are the ones that grow in abundance and have long been relied on by locals. They are the staples of a varied and (mostly) healthy Mediterranean diet.

MY TYRRHENIAN LARDER

ALMONDS

Sicilian almonds are typically harvested between July and September, but their white, pink-tinged blossom appears in March; the almond-scented air announcing the advent of spring. Almonds were brought to the Tyrrhenian by the Greeks from central Asia; the main groves are in eastern Sicily in the Val di Noto and south-west near Agrigento, but almond trees are present all along the northern coast and on the islands of the Tyrrhenian. To harvest almonds, long rods are used knock them off the trees; the nut is then removed from the husk and they are left to dry in the sun for several days. They are either sold with their skins on or blanched in hot water to remove the skins, ready to be used raw in salads, in pasta sauces such as pesto trapanese, and as almond paste for delicately painted marzipan desserts. I always buy blanched almonds as I use them for baking and find the brown skin too bitter. I also usually have a packet of flaked almonds for tossing over salad and braised vegetables or through pasta.

ANCHOVIES

Anchovies are common throughout the Tyrrhenian and particularly in the waters abutting the coast of Campania in spring and summer. They are believed to be at their tastiest from March to May and are eaten fresh, fried, roasted or marinated, but the most common way is sotto sale o sott'olio (preserved in salt or oil), ancient methods for ensuring the sea's bounty is edible in the leaner winter months. Preserved anchovies lend a salty, umami flavour to many dishes and I often opt for a spoonful of anchovy paste to season a salsa verde, but do look out for anchovy fillets in glass jars preserved in oil. These can be tossed through pasta, draped over meat or eaten on toast with butter – a super easy and quick injection of flavour and saltiness.

BOTTARGA

Usually associated with Sardinia, bottarga (cured, dried fish roe) is also a speciality of the Tuscan town of Orbetello, famed for its bottarga di muggine – made from the eggs of female grey mullet. The Tuscan version is more delicate than its Sardinian counterpart. Bottarga may seem expensive, but it is only ever used sparingly as you don't need much to enjoy a salty, fishy hit of flavour. Sold in a dried block, it is generally vacuum packed, bright orange and a little soft, becoming harder and darker the longer you keep it. Once open, wrap it tightly and keep it in the fridge where it can sit happily for several months. To use bottarga, slice a piece off the end and pull off the thin outer layer of skin that preserves it, taking care to uncover only as much as you need. Bottarga can be grated over steamed vegetables dressed in olive oil, braised beans or simple buttery pasta. I also serve it in thin slices with a little olive oil and a squeeze of lemon, either on its own or on toast as an aperitivo.

BREADCRUMBS

In Italy you can buy tubs of pangrattato, which are very fine breadcrumbs used for sprinkling over pasta or coating vegetables, meat or balls of rice for deep-frying. Historically a staple of the cucina povera larder to avoid wasting stale bread, it was used in poorer cities such as Naples to mimic the texture of grated parmesan on pasta dishes. For the recipes in this book you can buy unflavoured fine breadcrumbs; however, homemade breadcrumbs are supremely easy to make and have the added benefit of being free (if you use bread you would otherwise throw away) with more flavour than shop bought. Just remove the crusts from a few slices of stale (at least a day old) bread and pulse in a food processor to the desired consistency – very fresh bread won't break down in the processor so dry it out in the oven first. Once you have your breadcrumbs, lightly toast them in a dry frying pan with salt for 5 minutes, tossing occasionally and drizzling with a little olive oil if you like. The consistency will vary according to the type of bread you use: sourdough or more rustic loaves will yield a coarser crumb, and white sliced will be much finer. It doesn't really matter – just use whatever you have. The breadcrumbs will keep in a dry, airtight container for a few weeks, or several months in the freezer.

CAPERS

Not many people realise that a caper is the plant's flower still in its bud. If left to mature rather than being harvested, it blooms into an elegant, almost tropical looking pink and white flower. Capers are a wonderful way to pep up any dish, elevating it to something more sophisticated. I have learnt that this goes way beyond scattering a handful of the small ones preserved in brine over grilled fish. Having tried the capers 'sotto sale' (in salt) in Salina, I now understand they are a whole other thing. Just as with olive oil in Tuscany, there are gradations of quality you may not be aware of unless you've been to these places – unlike the inhabitants of the Aeolian Islands, who have known for millennia. I really encourage you to be picky about which capers you buy, and where possible opt for those preserved in salt as the flavour is far more powerful and fragrant than the little buds in brine. You can find glass jars of salted capers in most supermarkets, or if you go to a caper-growing region such as Sicily you can usually find salted capers sotto vuoto (vacuum-packed). I buy these as they are easy to transport, and when I'm back in my kitchen I simply transfer the salted capers to a glass jar, where they sit quite happily for up to 12 months to be used as and when they are needed. Maurizia, who owns Sapori Eoliani where my favourite capers come from, says you must soak salted capers for at least six hours, changing their water three or four times, but I find that a couple of hours usually does the trick. Sapori Eoliani ship internationally if you want to taste the best.

DRIED CHILLIES

In Italian cooking chillies are used more for flavour and seasoning than to blow your head off. They are usually air-dried, then crushed and sold by the gram in little plastic bags. In Campania any alimentare (grocery store) will have bunches of chillies drying on the ceiling – a beautiful ornament to any room – and this carries on down south through Calabria and into Sicily. Calabrian cuisine is spicier than elsewhere, as illustrated by their fiery salami spread 'nduja and the incredibly hot chilli oils they sell by the side of the road. As with anything powerful, I would urge you to get to know your preferred chilli. When I was testing a recipe for chilli chocolate cake for my first book I happened to be in the UK so I used the (as it turns out, significantly milder) crushed chillies available in the supermarket; when I got home to Florence and made it with a pinch of chilli flakes I had bought in Campania everyone began coughing and spluttering the moment they took their first bite. If you can't find crushed chillies, you can buy whole dried ones and crush them yourself using a pestle and mortar or high-speed blender (open carefully so the spicy dust doesn't go in your eyes). They will keep indefinitely in an airtight container. Sprinkle over vegetables, use to pep up a tomato sauce or make one of my all-time favourite Neapolitan dishes: spaghetti aglio, olio e pepperoncino.

OLIVES FROM GAETA

Similar to Greek Kalamata olives, Gaeta olives are small and violet with compact, intensely flavoured flesh. Unlike olives harvested for oil (which usually happens in October and November), Gaeta olives for eating are picked in March and April when the fruit takes on the deep purple colour they are known for. I love including Gaeta olives in a pasta sauce such as penne alla buttera as they add an intense pop of flavour when you happen across one. They are also delicious served as an antipasto alongside a hunk of pecorino romano cheese. If you can't find Gaeta olives, then Greek Kalamata or Ligurian Taggiasca will do instead. I don't recommend buying tins of the black ones that have already been pitted as they won't bring much flavour to the party. For this reason, all the recipes in this book call for unpitted olives.

OREGANO

A popular staple in much Mediterranean and southern Italian cooking, oregano is a perennial plant that grows in temperate mountainous conditions. Its name has lovely Greek origins: coming from the words 'oros' (mountain) and 'ganos' (joy and brightness), the literal meaning is 'the joy of the mountain'. Fresh oregano leaves are velvety and less intense in flavour than dried so they are not so good to cook with. The craggy cliffs and mountains of Campania, Calabria, Sardinia and in particular Sicily provide the perfect conditions for oregano to thrive and it has long been foraged to flavour food. Short of foraging your own, dried oregano is sold in enormous bunches at market stalls and greengrocers throughout Italy. With its robust taste a little can go a long way, and you might find it difficult to buy just a small amount for a particular dish. If you do buy a large bunch you can pick the leaves and store them in a glass jar, ready to use when needed; that said, I find that the dried supermarket stuff works just fine in all of these recipes.

PISTACHIOS

Some of the best pistachios in the world are grown and cultivated on the slopes of Mount Etna in Bronte, meaning that pistachios play a key role in Sicilian cooking. The volcanic soil adds to the flavour, and pistachios from this region are characterised by their purple, pink and brown skins and bright green flesh. While they are usually used in sweets and baking, pistachios also make an occasional appearance in savoury Sicilian dishes, most commonly in pistachio pesto for pasta. But the star of the show is pistachio cream, which can be bought in glass jars at most stores and used to flavour ice-cream or fill Sicilian breakfast pastries – delicious but bound to send one straight into a food coma. When preparing pistachios, many recipes call for their outer skin to be removed, but I find this to be a bit of a hassle; the main benefit is that the colour will be a more intense green without the papery pinkish-brown skin.

TINNED TOMATOES AND PASSATA

It is important to be pragmatic as a cook, and in my opinion tinned tomatoes are one of the greatest culinary inventions of all time. I love them and often opt for them over fresh tomatoes as their flavour is more intense (particularly during the colder months of the year when tomatoes are not at their best). For best results buy tins of whole plum tomatoes, then break them up with a wooden spoon; I find the flavour of 'chopped' tomatoes simply isn't as good. I also find that chopped tomatoes stubbornly retain their shape and texture, while peeled plum tomatoes will disintegrate more easily into the sauce with vigorous mashing. I recommend buying the best quality you can afford – cheaper tins tend to be less sweet and more acidic – but if you do use a cheaper variety, simply simmer it for longer to cook the acidity away. While tinned tomatoes are my favourite, glass jars of passata are perfect for when you want a smooth, tomatoey consistency as they are just pureed and sieved tomatoes. It's preferable when making caponata, for example, as the aim is for the tomato flavour to help the other ingredients sing without being the main event.

MY TYRRHENIAN ORCHARD

AUBERGINES

Aubergines (or eggplants) came to Sicily with the Arabs and many varieties have been cultivated throughout Italy ever since, but especially on the island, which is still the largest producer of aubergines. My favourite variety is the round violet Sicilian one, called tonde: it has sweeter flesh than the usual dark purple one and develops a lovely creamy texture when cooked. Initially known as 'mela insana' (mad apple) Italians were very suspicious of aubergines as they cause indigestion if eaten in vast quantities. Campania is famous for the long, dark, skinny variety, which locals declare to be the only kind you can use to make a true melanzana parmigiana. When buying aubergines, make sure they feel firm and don't have any brown patches or bruises. Many recipes salt the aubergines first, as historically this was seen as the best way to rid them of their bitter flavour and draw out some of the moisture, making the flesh less spongy and likely to absorb less oil when cooking. I don't always find this necessary as aubergines have become less bitter due to mass cultivation, though they still benefit from salting if you are going to fry them as it makes them less greasy. (A restaurateur friend swears that putting them in the microwave for 10 minutes achieves the same thing.)

LEMONS

A world without bright, citrusy lemons would be hard to imagine. The culinary symbol of Campania and Sicily, their scent and even appearance evoke romantic coastlines, salty sea air and mandolins. Romance aside, lemons are also incredibly versatile, suitable for both sweet and savoury cooking. As with most ingredients, sourcing them first-hand makes a big difference and the freshly plucked lemons you find along the Amalfi Coast, Sorrento or on the Sicilian islands will elevate any dish to dizzying heights of fabulousness. They are so unacidic that on Capri lemons are sliced and eaten raw, dressed with a little olive oil, salt and parsley as a salad. If you can, buy unwaxed imported lemons from these regions – they will be large and knobbly, grown on terraces with little or no pesticides, and may even still have a couple of beautiful leaves attached. I have seen crates of these at a few greengrocers in London. If you can't find them aim for organic unwaxed lemons (to be organic they have to be unwaxed) as you'll usually want the zest or peel – not an appealing prospect when waxed with polyethylene or shellac, although this matters less if you're only using the juice.

TOMATOES

One of Italy's most emblematic ingredients, tomatoes were brought over to Europe from America by the Spanish in the Middle Ages, but didn't make their way into people's kitchens for another two centuries or so. A symbol of Campania, the San Marzano is a bright-red plum tomato that thrives in the mineral-rich soil surrounding Vesuvius and Naples. These beautiful tomatoes are sweet rather than acidic; they're very well suited to cooking and are perfect for eating raw in a salad during the summer. However, if I am eating tomatoes out of season, I will always buy datterini cherry tomatoes as these miniature morsels are far tastier than their watery hothouse counterparts sold in supermarkets during winter. I find that the best way to bring out the flavour of tomatoes is by sprinkling them with a little salt about five minutes before serving, then drizzling with a little olive oil – never with any pepper or balsamic vinegar. I always use this method when I'm preparing them for a salad as it makes them taste their most 'tomatoey'.

ZUCCHINI

Zucchini (or courgettes) are inextricably linked to summer as they grow with unstoppable vigour and often have to be given away by the crateload. Or so says my uncle, who lives in Catalonia; he has such a glut of zucchini in his vegetable patch that he despairs of what to do with them, and has nightmares about 'the ones that lurk under a large leaf and suddenly poke their three-foot heads out'. I love zucchini in all their guises and the myriad of ways they can be prepared. I adore the variety on display at market stalls come summer, so different from the ubiquitous dark green zucchini lunghe sold in supermarkets across the world, all year round. The warmer months bring the lovely hexagonal pale-green type, bright-yellow ones the colour of egg yolk, and those that are so pale they remind me of eggshell. One such favourite are baby zucchini, which are delicious steamed and tossed with lemon juice, olive oil, basil, salt and pepper, served alongside balls of buffalo mozzarella. You could also leave out the basil and mozzarella and grate a little bottarga over the top.

MY TYRRHENIAN FRIDGE

BUFFALO MOZZARELLA

This dense, porcelain-white, slightly tangy, fresh cheese is made exclusively in Campania from the milk of the black water buffalo that roam the plains of Salerno and Caserta. If you drive along the main road from Salerno to the national park of Cilento in Campania, you will see a sign for a different mozzarella producer every hundred metres – though, as with everything, there are mozzarella producers and there are mozzarella producers. According to our friend Antonella, who owns a lovely B&B (Il Cannito) near Paestum, the nearby Tenuta Vannullo is one of only a handful of organic mozzarella farms, where the buffalo are treated like royalty. At any time, three-quarters of the herd will be out grazing on mineral-rich volcanic grass, while the rest are in large barns for milking. The spacious barns are equipped with massage machines the buffalo can operate themselves to have their backs rubbed and they are played classical music for two hours in the early morning. The milk is extracted using the latest self-milking machines, which allow the buffalo to enter voluntarily when they feel their udders need emptying. So efficient is this system that, as we watched, the buffalo were forming an orderly queue to patiently wait their turn for milking. Buffalo mozzarella has a protected DOP (designation of origin) status, meaning that its production is closely scrutinised by the Consortium, which regularly checks up on its hundred and fifty or so producers. Among other things, they keep an eye on the size as the largest balls of buffalo mozzarella cannot exceed 800 g (1 lb 12 oz) in weight or they must be called something else. I love to eat mozzarella in the same way I eat tomatoes – dressed simply with olive oil and a sprinkle of sea salt. It's a fabulous pairing with a myriad of vegetables: steamed baby zucchini, a simple tomato salad or with a few slices of prosciutto di Parma. If you happen to buy mozzarella directly from a producer in Campania though, the taste will be so fresh, tangy and moreish that you won't actually need to dress it in anything at all.

PECORINO ROMANO

Pecorino romano is a strong white sheep's cheese, now world-famous as the main component of cacio e pepe sauce. As another product with protected DOP (designation of origin) status it can only be produced in the regions of Lazio, Sardinia and the province of Grosseto along the southern Tuscan coast. Pecorino romano has been made exclusively with milk from sheep who have grazed in the open pastures in these provinces for over two millennia. In Ancient Rome it was considered the perfect condiment at Imperial court, and was included in the ration packs of Rome's marching armies as it was believed to be easily digestible and high in energy-giving qualities. Its health benefits are reflected in the life expectancy of shepherds in Sardinia, where most pecorino romano is produced – Sardinia is the world's first declared 'Blue Zone', meaning that its inhabitants consistently live into their hundredth year. I often leave a hunk of this pungent salty cheese on the table during drinks o'clock so that people can hack away at it while sipping a glass of something.

RICOTTA

Ricotta is not a cheese but a by-product of the cheese-making process. It is made from the liquid (whey) left over after milk has been heated to separate the curds for making mozzarella, pecorino and so on. Once the curds are removed the whey is reheated and a softer, grainier solid forms, which is then packed into the conical-shaped tubs that give ricotta its distinctive shape. I always keep a tub of ricotta in the fridge as it lends itself to quick last-minute cooking and easy snacks to serve with drinks when I have people over. Its soft texture and mellow flavour also work well in sweet dishes and I have included two of my favourite Campanian dishes in the Dolci section. If you happen to be near a cheesemaker with fresh ricotta, this is delicious served alongside vegetables and salads for a light lunch, dressed simply with a little salt, pepper and olive oil, but generally the UHT ricotta available in most supermarkets is absolutely fine in these recipes. Whatever ricotta you use, remember to first drain it in a colander over the sink for at least five minutes to remove the excess liquid.

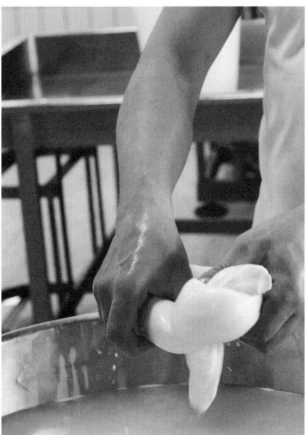
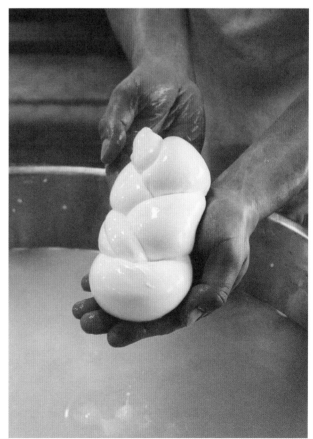

PRODUCE AND INGREDIENTS FROM THE TYRRHENIAN

I MENÚ

MENUS

A FEW FAVOURITE LUNCHES

❦ ❦ ❦ *Serve all at once, for everyone to help themselves*

MENU #1

TO START:–

Fusilli with pistachio pesto and lemon zest ... **p. 106**

Grilled zucchini or aubergine with garlic and chilli ... **p. 186**

Roast peppers with salsa verde and burrata ... **p. 70**

TO FINISH:–

Raspberry tiramisu ... **p. 204**

MENU #2

TO START:–

Crostini with spicy 'nduja salami, ricotta and basil ... **p. 57**

Calamarata pasta with aubergine, olives, pecorino romano and almonds ... **p. 92**

Garlicky grilled tomatoes ... **p. 176**

TO FINISH:–

Summery cherry tart ... **p. 210**

MENU #3

TO START:–

Baked aubergine and ricotta sformato with tomato sauce ... **p. 86**

Grilled zucchini with garlic and chilli ... **p. 186**

Green salad with olive oil and white wine vinegar ... **p. 174**

TO FINISH:–

Ricotta and cinnamon sfogliatella pie with orange salad ... **p. 216**

MENU #4

TO START:–

Zucchini, mint and bechamel lasagne ... **p. 108**

Green salad with olive oil and white wine vinegar ... **p. 174**

TO FINISH:–

Flourless lemon and almond cake with chocolate ganache ... **p. 225**

MENU #1

TO START:–

Viviana's acquacotta ... **p. 88**

TO FINISH:–

Fig, walnut and sweet wine cake ... **p. 222**

MENU #2

TO START:–

Penne with cowboy ragu ... **p. 156**

Green salad with olive oil and white wine vinegar ... **p. 174**

TO FINISH:–

Pistachio panna cotta with raspberries ... **p. 202**

MENU #3

TO START:–

'My' spaghetti with zucchini and basil ... **p. 95**

TO FINISH:–

Lemon tiramisu ... **p. 205**

MENU #4

TO START:–

Silvana's saffron fish risotto with red mullet ragu ... **p. 124**

TO FINISH:–

Raspberry tiramisu ... **p. 204**

MINIMAL COOKING FOR HOT DAYS AND NIGHTS

MENU #1

TO START:–

Rigatoni with fiery roast tomatoes and ricotta ... **p. 105**

TO FINISH:–

Lemon granita ... **p. 200**

MENU #2

TO START:–

Grilled tuna steaks with fresh peas and salsa verde ... **p. 139**

Hasselback 'hedgehog' potatoes ... **p. 188**

TO FINISH:–

Pistachio panna cotta ... **p. 202**

MENU #3

TO START:–

Beef carpaccio with zucchini, rocket and pecorino ... **p. 159**

Garlicky grilled tomatoes ... **p. 176**

Maurizia's potato, olive and caper salad ... **p. 84**

TO FINISH:–

Pistachio granita ... **p. 201**

MENU #4

TO START:–

Whole sea bream cooked 'in parcels' with lemon, thyme and olives ... **p. 140**

Garlicky grilled tomatoes ... **p. 176**

TO FINISH:–

Lemon tiramisu ... **p. 205**

A FEW FAVOURITE FEASTS TO IMPRESS

QUICK DISHES TO MAKE 'AL VOLO'

✹ ✹ ✹ *Ready in 45 minutes or less*

✚ ✚ ✚ *These recipes are not quick, but can be made in stages when you have time*

Caponata with buffalo mozzarella . . . **p. 81**
Can be made the day before – just remove from the fridge 30 minutes before serving.

Zucchini, mint and bechamel lasagne . . . **p. 108**
Can be assembled ahead – just remove from the fridge and bake as instructed in the recipe; if cooking from frozen, add 15 minutes to the baking time.

Baked aubergine with pasta, mozzarella and tomatoes . . . **p. 110**
Can be assembled ahead – just remove from the fridge and bake as instructed in the recipe.

Mussel soup with tomatoes, parsley and garlic . . . **p. 136**
You can make the tomato sauce for the soup up to 3 days ahead and keep it in a sealed container in the fridge. When ready to serve, heat up and cook the mussels as instructed in the recipe.

Ricotta gnocchi in tomato and mozzarella sauce . . . **p. 152**
You can make the gnocchi and tomato sauce the day before and bring them together just before serving.

Ricotta, pear and hazelnut biscuit cake . . . **p. 212**
Poach the pears the day before assembling to save on cooling time. You can also make the sandwich discs the day before and keep them in an airtight container.

Amalfi lemon cream cake . . . **p. 227**
Eliminate cooling time on the day of serving by making the lemon curd up to 3 days ahead and keeping it in an airtight container in the fridge. The sponges may also be made up to 3 days ahead, wrapped and seal in an airtight container. Assemble the cake a minimum of 3 hours before serving or the day before.

Rosemary and honey fritters . . . **p. 206**
The dough can be made ahead of time and kept in the fridge for up to 3 days, or in the freezer indefinitely.

Pavlova with passion fruit curd . . . **p. 229**
You can make the curd and meringue up to 3 days before serving and assemble at the last minute. If anything goes wrong, remember that a passion fruit 'Eton mess' is just as delicious as a pavlova.

Summery cherry tart . . . **p. 210**
Ricotta and cinnamon sfogliatella pie with orange salad . . . **p. 216**
You can make the pastry ahead of time and keep in the fridge for up to 3 days or freeze indefinitely. Or roll out the pastry and store it in the tart case; it bakes very well from frozen.

BEFORE THE MEAL

L'APERITIVO

L'APERITIVO

The aperitivo in Italy is a serious business, a sacred ritual of stimulating the appetite before dinner. It is also universal: whether you are drinking an expensive cocktail at a swanky hotel or sipping a beer straight from the bottle in your local bar, tradition dictates that any drink after 6 pm must be accompanied by something delicious to eat, often rather a lot of delicious somethings. There is a saying: 'l'appetito viene mangiando' (appetite comes with eating) so many bars often offer a wonderful selection of nibbles to get you going before the evening meal. Many a student has sustained themselves with these titbits; for the €5 they spend on their Campari Spritz (prosecco over ice with a good glug of Campari and a splash of soda – heaven) they can gorge themselves on nuts, bruschette, crostini and slices of thick rustic pizza. I adore aperitivo hour and have included some of my favourite drinks and snacks to enjoy at cocktail o'clock. Aside from the fact that it reminds me of happy evenings in Italy, it's also an easy way to feed a crowd as you can usually pre-prepare a selection of snacks leaving you free to chat to friends over drinks. If you make it abundant enough you cut out the need for a first course; after a crostino with 'nduja and ricotta, a slice of pizzetta with lemon and thyme, and a few handfuls of salted almonds or squares of chickpea panelle you can happily go straight into the main course without feeling hard done by.

OPPOSITE:– Beer and lemon granita shandy and Chickpea fritters with parsley and lemon (see pages 46 and 48).

Pesche con vino bianco

PEACHES IN WHITE WINE

This is hardly a recipe – more a decadent combination of flavours that immediately transports me to sun-soaked days in the tiny bay of Laurito, just around the corner from Positano. This is home to the famous beach shack restaurant Da Adolfo (only reachable by boat), where everyone is served a large jug of white wine with peaches before lunch. But it's not just at Da Adolfo that you find it: in my native Tuscany, fruit sellers at our local Saturday food market ask anyone buying a bag of peaches, 'Ma, da mangiare or per il vino?' (To eat or to soak in wine?) to gauge the maturity and quality of the peaches required. Some people drink the wine first, saving the peach slices for dessert. I like to sip the wine with the fruit bumping up against my lips and occasionally fish out a piece to munch on. Summer in a glass.

PREPARATION:– 5 minutes, plus chilling time

SERVES 4

3 ripe but firm yellow peaches
1 bottle dry white wine
ice cubes, to serve

Cut the peaches in half, removing and discarding the stones. Slice each half into three or four segments, depending on size – you want them to be small enough to eat in one mouthful. As you go, put the slices in a serving jug.

When you've finished, pour the wine into the jug, then place in the fridge to chill and infuse for at least 3 hours.

Serve in wine glasses over a few cubes of ice. Drink immediately.

Limoncello spritz

PROSECCO, LIMONCELLO AND BASIL COCKTAIL

This light citrusy spritz has been popping up all along the coast over the past decade, particularly in Sicily. Apart from being a beautiful colour and wonderfully refreshing, it's also a good way to use up prosecco or limoncello, which I often have lying around. It's important to get the balance right – too much limoncello will make it too tart and alcoholic; what you're aiming for is a subtle citrus note within a glass of dry prosecco. Now that I've discovered how easy and delicious it is to make homemade limoncello (see page 232) I'll often use my own here, but shop bought is also fine. My only word of caution would be to add less as it can taste more synthetic and throw the balance off; start with half the amount recommended below and taste before adding any more to make sure it's not too sweet.

PREPARATION:– 5 minutes

SERVES 6

ice cubes, to serve

handful of basil leaves

90 ml (3 fl oz) homemade or shop-bought limoncello

1 bottle good-quality dry prosecco

soda water, to taste

6 lemon slices

Fill a glass with plenty of ice and a few basil leaves. Pour over 15 ml (½ fl oz) of limoncello, followed by about 125 ml (4 fl oz) of prosecco and a splash of soda water. Gently stir to combine. Add a slice of lemon to the glass and garnish with a few more basil leaves. Repeat to make six cocktails (or increase the quantities and make as many as you like).

VARIATIONS

WHITE SPRITZ:– Pour prosecco over ice. Add a splash of soda water, a strip of lemon peel and a sprig of mint.

SPRITZ ALLE MORE:– Place a scoop of Blackberry granita (see page 198) in a glass and pour over an equal measure of prosecco.

L'APERITIVO

BEER AND LEMON GRANITA SHANDY

This is served from the shack bar on Scario beach on the island of Salina. Messina is the most ubiquitous brand of lager in Sicily, named after the port town in the north-east of the island. When you order your 'Messina sporca' or 'dirty Messina beer' you are given a glass that is almost completely full of icy lemony granita over which you pour your beer little by little. It's everything you want on a hot summer's day: citrusy, cold and slightly bitter and fizzy from the beer. I now make it for friends whenever it's hot as it stays cold and means that your beer takes longer to drink. You can use any size glass; the important thing to remember is the ratio of 3 parts granita to 1 part beer (hence the gradual topping up described in the method) as you want the lovely lemony flavour rather than a full glass of beer with a little lemony ice floating in it. The drink should be predominantly granita topped with beer.

PREPARATION:– 5 minutes, plus standing time

SERVES 4

about 400 g (14 oz) Lemon granita (see page 200)

4 x 330 ml (11 fl oz) bottles Messina beer (or other light lager)

Remove the granita from the freezer 5 minutes before serving to allow it to soften slightly.

Line up four tall glasses and spoon in the lemon granita until each glass is almost full, leaving a little space for the beer. Serve each glass with an open bottle of Messina and allow the drinker to slowly pour the beer over the granita to the top of the glass. Drink immediately, topping up with beer as required.

NOTE:– Pictured on page 40

SALTED ALMONDS

Part of the glamour of La Dolce Vita is the white-coated Italian waiter, whose job it is to charm the guests at whatever high-end bar, restaurant or hotel terrace they are serving in. I am thinking in particular of the bar terrace at the Grand Hotel Excelsior Vittoria in Sorrento, or the Santa Caterina just outside Amalfi – both grand old dames of the hotel world where you don't have to be a resident to sip a perfect gin martini in front of the most astonishing sea views. I always stop for a drink at the Santa Caterina when I'm in the area and am beyond thrilled when the waiter remembers the first drink I ordered there, and exactly how I like it (a gin and tonic with lots of lime juice and angostura bitters).

One of my favourite tropes of these glamorous spots is the simple but very stylish aperitivo. Usually served in a Belle Époque silver dish with three compartments, it contains the following: giant green olives; crunchy and salty crisps (definitely a cut above standard potato chips); and salted almonds. Honestly, I am more excited by this selection than by any plate of bruschetta or cheese. I now make my own salted almonds to serve alongside the best olives and crisps I can get my hands on to transport myself and my guests to the Santa Caterina.

PREPARATION:– 10 minutes, plus cooling time
COOKING:– 10 minutes

MAKES 1 LARGE JAR

1 large organic egg white
2 teaspoons fine sea salt
400 g (14 oz) blanched almonds
flaky sea salt

Preheat the oven to 200°C (400°F) fan-forced. Line two baking trays with baking parchment.

Using a fine mesh strainer, sieve the egg white into a small bowl to get rid of the stringy bits. Whisk with a small whisk or fork for a few seconds until a little frothy. Add the salt and whisk for a few more moments, then mix through the almonds, making sure they are well coated.

Pour the almonds onto the prepared trays and spread out in a single layer. Roast for 10 minutes or until they start to smell nutty.

Remove from the oven and sprinkle liberally with flaky sea salt, then leave to cool completely. Serve in a small bowl alongside some giant green olives, salted crisps and whatever you fancy to drink. They accompany a martini very well. Store any leftovers in an airtight container for up to 2 weeks.

NOTE:– Pictured on page 44

Panelle con prezzemolo e limone

CHICKPEA FRITTERS WITH PARSLEY AND LEMON

These incredibly moreish chickpea flour fritters are a stalwart of Palermitano street food. They are said to be a legacy left on Sicily by the Arabs, although variations of the dish can be found throughout the Mediterranean – Genovese farinata, Livorno's torta di ceci and the Provencal socca are all similar. In Palermo they hold a special place in the city's culinary tradition, and Palermitani have found ingenious ways to shape and slice the panelle mixture as thinly as possible before it is fried to yield the crunchiest, most delicious results. My favourite comes from the current Duchess of Palma, a famously proficient cook and daughter-in-law of Giuseppe Tomasi di Lampedusa, author of the wonderful Sicilian novel *The Leopard*. She presses the chickpea mixture into an empty tin of tomatoes with the ends removed, puts it in the fridge for a few hours and then pushes the hardened mixture out, cutting slices with a piece of wire to achieve perfectly thin, round slices for frying.

On the streets of Palermo, panelle are prepared in dedicated shops or market stalls known as friggitorie (frying shops) and are often eaten in a sandwich by anyone craving a particularly stodgy meal. Personally, I like them on their own with a little lemon juice to accompany a cold beer or glass of wine. They can be eaten cold, although they are best eaten soon after cooking. I'm aware that most Palermitani would consider this sacrilege, but I prefer to bake the mixture – it's less labour intensive than frying and yields a lighter snack. That said, if you have the patience and the appetite, do as the Sicilians do and fry away!

PREPARATION:– 20 minutes, plus cooling time
COOKING:– 25 minutes

150 g (5½ oz) chickpea flour
(gram flour)

½ teaspoon fine sea salt

handful of finely chopped
flat-leaf parsley

50 ml (1¾ fl oz) olive oil

flaky sea salt, grated lemon
zest and lemon juice, to serve

Put the chickpea flour and salt in a medium saucepan, stirring with a whisk to remove any lumps and make sure the salt is evenly distributed. Gradually start adding 450 ml (15 fl oz) water, in small batches of about 100 ml (3½ fl oz), whisking as you go to combine without forming lumps. When the mixture becomes more liquid, you can whisk in the rest of the water.

Put the pan over a medium heat and continue to whisk as the flour cooks and thickens. The process is rather like making polenta; you need to whisk constantly in the same direction for 5 minutes or so until the mixture is thick and dense and starting to come away from the side. Stir in the parsley.

Line a large chopping board with baking parchment. Pour the mixture onto it, then use a knife to spread it almost to the edges of the board, flattening it out to an even thickness of around 1 cm (½ inch). Cool slightly. Top with a second piece of parchment and, being careful not to squash it too much, gently smooth it out with a rolling pin. Place in the fridge and leave to cool for around 20 minutes (or longer if you are not cooking the panelle until much later).

Preheat the oven to 220°C (425°F) fan-forced.

Remove the top layer of paper and transfer to a large plate. Using a large, sharp knife, cut the mixture into 3 cm (1¼ inch) squares, making them as uniform as you can manage. (You could also use a square or rectangular cookie cutter if you have one.) Set the panelle aside on the lined plate. Gather up any leftover mixture, flatten it between sheets of baking parchment as above, and shape so that you don't waste any.

Take a baking tray large enough to fit all the panelle and line with baking parchment. Using either a pastry brush or your fingers, brush a little olive oil over both sides of each square and place on the lined tray. Bake for 20 minutes or until the tops are crisp and the sides begin to curl.

Transfer the panelle to a serving plate, scatter with some flaky sea salt and lemon zest, and finish with a generous squeeze of lemon juice.

NOTE:– Pictured on page 40

TOSCANA: LA MAREMMA

 When people think of Tuscany, they rarely picture the sea. And yet Tuscany has one of Italy's longest coastlines, the southern stretch of which is known as Maremma – a wide expanse of marshland that separates the mountains from the sea. The wooded mountains of inland Tuscany give way to wide-open expanses of gentle rolling hills dotted with olive trees, at which point you know that the sea isn't far away. All roads lead to Rome, and the one from Siena along the coast is called the Via Aurelia, which thrills and delights at every turn. Aurelia is the feminine for the Roman Aurelius, derived from 'golden', alluding to the wheat fields lining the road that blaze with colour in high summer. Long avenues of umbrella pines separate the coast from the road, alerting you to the proximity of the beach.

This stretch of coastline has been inhabited for millennia. The buzzing town of Orbetello, which sits on the lagoon connecting the island-like promontory of Monte Argentario, was originally an Etruscan settlement. The mighty city walls, still very much standing, were built in the 5th century BCE. The Etruscans began work on the city cathedral, but this was taken over by the Romans when they took control of Orbetello and the local area in the 5th century CE. Its Gothic facade was added a thousand years later in the 14th century.

Every year, Orbetello hosts a food festival to coincide with All Souls' Day on 1 November. The town is dotted with stands showcasing fresh produce and making local recipes, as well as dishes from the surrounding area and nearby islands.

The food of Maremma is a mixture of land and sea. I met a man from Ansedonia who described it as having a choice between two restaurants on either side of the road: if you choose the side hugging the coast, the menu will consist entirely of fish; cross over to the inland side and you will be offered dishes made with beans, chestnuts, wild boar, rabbit and even snails – minestra di lumache (snail stew) features on many stands at the food fair.

Snails aside, the food of this area is similar to the agricultural cucina povera I grew up with. Many Maremman dishes can be found throughout Tuscany and beyond, such as ravioli Maremmani (the now-ubiquitous ravioli stuffed with spinach and ricotta) and cinghiale in umido (wild boar stew). But there are also local dishes that you can only really find in the Maremma, such as acquacotta (vegetable soup with eggs poached in it) and pasta alla buttera, a meat ragu named after local butteri, cowboys who historically wrangled the buffalo that roamed the coastal marshes. The famous British-born writer and wartime diarist Iris Origo had a connection to this nearby stretch of coast as her father-in-law was from the area. In the now-famous gardens she built at her home, La Foce, there is a sculpture of several butteri on horseback, struggling to herd these enormous horned beasts through the marshes.

This combination of land and sea is very different from the rocky stretches of the Tyrrhenian further south in Campania; in Maremma, the beaches are sandy and the waters shallow, making a bucket-and-spade day an uncomplicated affair. The only task is to haul yourself along the beach to a restaurant for lunch. For as long as I can remember one such favourite has been the Carmen Bay restaurant on a stretch of beach known as Macchiatonda, a short drive off the Aurelia beyond the train tracks that hug the coast. The restaurant is simple and easy going, though there is a rule of thumb when ordering: choose pasta and it will arrive in five minutes; order fish and you will be waiting for hours. I never mind this as I usually eat a plate of pasta while waiting for the fish. After all, if the sun is shining and there is a crisp glass of wine to be sipped, what's the rush?

Another heavenly spot a little further north up the coast is Ansedonia, a beach sheltered by a large headland. Every year we make a pilgrimage to this beach with our great friend Beatrix and a painter friend named Tom. There's nothing there except a tiny shack selling sandwiches and piping-hot coffee, though a short wander down the beach leads to another favourite eatery, La Strega, which makes a mean frittura di mare (calamari and prawns fried in a light crispy batter, served with a wedge of lemon), spaghetti con bottarga and salt-baked wild sea bass from the Tuscan archipelago. If you visit in May there will be no one on the beach, except perhaps for a keen treasure hunter, snorkelling with a waterproof metal detector looking for who knows what. The water will be cold, but the promontory and grass leading to the beach is thick with poppies and spring wildflowers. A very different story from summer, when the beach is filled with families cooling down from the oppressive heat. In the evenings we would often take a trip up to the hilltop town of Capalbio, which stands like a beacon overlooking the Maremma, with its battlements and gorgeous views, the blue and pink light casting long shadows across the undulating landscape.

Down the road is one of the most surprising additions to the Maremma: the Tarot Garden of Niki de Saint Phalle. The French surrealist sculptor built this bizarre playground on a patch of hillside gifted to her by Carlo and Nicola Caracciolo. Photographs often make it look kitsch and tacky, but in real life it's like a fantasy land brought to life. Building-sized, mosaiced sculptures represent the cards from a tarot reading. Some of the sculptures have in fact served as buildings – the most impressive being a giant blue sphinx with stairs up to her back from where you can see the sea, and inside De Saint Phalle's own apartment, including a bedroom, bathroom, kitchen and dining room, all covered floor to ceiling in mirror shards. The dazzling effect eventually forced Saint Phalle to move out as she felt it was driving her mad. I have visited the open-air museum with artist friends who say it completely changed their outlook and scope of ambition for their own work.

This is the charm of the Maremma: it's a slow-burn, surprising place whose appeal grows on you by degrees. Unlike the southern Tyrrhenian, with its dramatic landscapes that virtually smack you in the face, the land here is flat, calm and undulating. The train chuffs along the coastal train track, buffalos mosey across fields, and the sea laps gently onto sandy beaches. With its ethereal feel and ambiguous quality, there are few more meditative experiences than looking out to sea from the southernmost point of Tuscany.

Crostini con ricotta, limone e salvia

CROSTINI WITH RICOTTA, LEMON AND CRUNCHY SAGE

A friend made a version of these crostini when we were staying at her house near Capalbio on Tuscany's southern coast. I remember being struck by how aromatic and delicate they were, but with a punch coming from the chilli flakes, along with the clashing textures of soft ricotta and crunchy sage. An optional (but delicious) addition is to drape an anchovy over the ricotta before finishing with the sage leaves. The perfect aperitivo on a warm evening with a cold glass of prosecco.

PREPARATION:– 10 minutes
COOKING:– 10 minutes

SERVES 6

6 large slices of white sourdough (preferably a little stale), cut 1 cm (½ inch) thick

250 g (12½ oz) tub ricotta, drained

grated zest of 2 lemons

pinch of chilli flakes

sea salt and freshly ground black pepper

70 ml (2¼ fl oz) olive oil, plus extra for drizzling

24–30 sage leaves

1 garlic clove, peeled and sliced in half

Preheat the oven to 150°C (300°F) fan-forced.

Cut the bread to your preferred size (it will be too brittle once it's been toasted) and arrange on a baking tray. Toast in the oven for 5–7 minutes, turning halfway through, until golden and completely dry. Remove the crostini from the oven and set aside until ready to serve.

In a bowl, combine the ricotta, lemon zest, chilli flakes, salt and pepper with a fork. You can prepare this mixture and the crostini several hours before assembling if you like. Cover and store in the fridge until you are ready to serve.

Pour the olive oil into a wide frying pan and heat over a medium heat for a minute or so until sizzling. Add the sage leaves in a single layer and fry for 30–40 seconds. As soon as the edges begin to curl and crisp up, remove the leaves with a slotted spoon or tongs – don't leave them any longer or they will become bitter. Drain on a plate lined with paper towel and sprinkle generously with salt.

Rub the crostini tops with the garlic halves and drizzle with a little extra olive oil. Place a heaped tablespoon of the ricotta mixture on each crostino and finish with another drizzle of olive oil. Top with four or five crispy sage leaves (depending on the size) and serve immediately with a glass of fizz.

Crostini con mascarpone, broccoli e peperoncino

CROSTINI WITH MASCARPONE, BROCCOLI AND CHILLI

A fabulous green crostino inspired by the fertile land surrounding Naples, where brassica grow in abundance. I suggest using tenderstem broccoli in the recipe as I love the flavour, but you can use regular broccoli if that's what you have – just chop it into manageable chunks before blanching.

PREPARATION:– 10 minutes
COOKING:– 10 minutes

SERVES 6

6 large slices of white sourdough (preferably a little stale), cut 1 cm (½ inch) thick

200 g (7 oz) broccoli, cut into florets

juice of ½ lemon

4 tablespoons olive oil

chilli flakes, to taste

sea salt and freshly ground black pepper

1 garlic clove, peeled and sliced in half

100 g (3½ oz) mascarpone

12 anchovy fillets (optional)

Preheat the oven to 150°C (300°F) fan-forced.

Cut the bread to your preferred size (it will be too brittle once it's been toasted) and arrange on a baking tray. Toast in the oven for 5–7 minutes, turning halfway through, until golden and completely dry. Remove the crostini from the oven and set aside until ready to serve.

Meanwhile, bring a medium saucepan of salted water to the boil. Blanch the broccoli for 4–5 minutes until tender but still retaining some texture, then drain and finely chop. Place in a bowl to cool slightly, then toss through the lemon juice, half the olive oil, a pinch of chilli flakes, a generous pinch of salt and a grind of pepper.

Rub the crostini tops with the garlic halves and drizzle with a little olive oil. Spread generously with mascarpone and sprinkle over some salt. Top with a heaped tablespoon of the dressed broccoli and drape over a couple of anchovy fillets, if using.

Place all the crostini on a large plate and serve immediately.

Crostini con 'nduja, ricotta e basilico

CROSTINI WITH SPICY 'NDUJA SALAMI, RICOTTA AND BASIL

'Nduja is a spicy salami spread from Calabria, the toe of the boot of Italy in the southernmost part of the Tyrrhenian Sea. It has an intense flavour that is often enjoyed simply spread on bread or spooned onto a pizza. The vivid red paste pairs beautifully with the fresh, silky taste and bright white colour of ricotta, and I love to pile this combination on crostini as a supremely easy pre-dinner snack for friends. The basil leaf adds a fragrant note as well as completing the colours of the Italian flag, which adds a little kitsch fun to proceedings.

PREPARATION:– 10 minutes
COOKING:– 10 minutes

SERVES 6

6 large slices of white sourdough (preferably a little stale), cut 1 cm (½ inch) thick

100 g (3½ oz) ricotta, drained

sea salt and freshly ground black pepper

3 tablespoons olive oil

50 g (1¾ oz) 'nduja

6 basil leaves

Preheat the oven to 150°C (300°F) fan-forced.

Cut the bread to your preferred size (it will be too brittle once it's been toasted) and arrange on a baking tray. Toast in the oven for 5–7 minutes, turning halfway through, until golden and completely dry. Remove the crostini from the oven and set aside until ready to serve.

Scoop the ricotta into a bowl, season with salt and pepper and mix with a fork. You can prepare this mixture and the crostini several hours before assembling. Cover and store in the fridge until you are ready to serve.

Drizzle each crostino with a little olive oil and a sprinkling of salt. Top with a tablespoon of seasoned ricotta, smoothing it out to the edges with the back of the spoon. Use a teaspoon to dollop the 'nduja onto the ricotta and spread it out. This isn't an exact science; you want roughly twice the amount of ricotta to 'nduja. Finish with a basil leaf and serve.

LEMON, MOZZARELLA AND THYME PIZZETTE

This is an interpretation of the incredible grilled mozzarella and lemon leaves from Da Adolfo in Positano. At this wonderful beach shack restaurant large lemon leaves are placed on the grill with glorious slices of fresh Campania mozzarella on top, lightly melting the cheese and infusing it with a lemony aroma. A huge part of the magic is the ingredients – the Amalfi lemon leaves plucked that morning from the tree and the freshest mozzarella you can get – and of course summer sunshine and the view of the Tyrrhenian add to the experience.

When I'm at home I like to recreate the flavours in the form of pizza slices to be shared as an aperitivo with a drink before dinner. Nowadays you can get very good pizza dough at the supermarket, so I often just buy that as this isn't ever the main event; just a nice citrusy something to nibble on. That said, if you would like to make your own dough, by all means do. I always use Hugh Fearnley-Whittingstall's 'perfect pizza dough' recipe (widely available online) to get the lightest, crispiest results. If you make your own, just adjust the recipe to however much dough you have, allowing about 110 grams (4 oz) per pizza. Whichever dough you use, take it out of the fridge or freezer at least an hour beforehand to bring it to temperature. Frozen dough may need an extra 10–15 minutes for the gluten to relax.

PREPARATION:– 40 minutes
COOKING:– 1 hour 10 minutes

3 lemons, finely sliced into 3 mm (⅛ inch) thick discs, ends discarded

1 tablespoon caster sugar

sea salt and freshly ground black pepper

plain flour, for dusting

about 880 g (1 lb 15 oz) pizza dough

4 large balls of fior di latte mozzarella, torn

handful of thyme sprigs, leaves picked

chilli flakes, to taste

grated zest of 2 lemons

Preheat the oven to 150°C (300°F) fan-forced. Line a baking tray with baking parchment.

Cut the lemon slices into quarter wedges, removing any pips as you go. Place on the prepared tray, allowing a little space in between. Lightly sprinkle each slice with sugar and salt, then place in the oven for 15 minutes until the lemon slices dry out and begin to curl up at the edges.

Meanwhile, lightly dust a baking tray with flour. Divide the pizza dough into eight even portions, folding the edges over and tucking them underneath to make a neat ball. Place each ball on the floured baking tray.

Remove the lemons from the oven and increase the temperature to 250°C (500°F) or as hot as it will go. Lightly flour two more baking trays and place in the oven while you prepare the pizza.

Drain the mozzarella and tear into very small pieces with your fingers. Leave in a colander in the sink for 5 minutes to drain off any excess liquid.

Lightly flour a clean work surface and place one ball of pizza dough on it. Use your middle three fingers to push down into the centre of the dough, then with those fingers keep pushing outwards to stretch the dough, using the other hand to rotate it so it flattens out evenly – don't use a rolling pin or you will push out all of the air. When it becomes quite wide and flat, lift and hold it by the edges in your hands, rotating it and allowing gravity to pull it down and stretch it. You want it to be about 24 cm (9½ inch) wide and 1 cm (½ inch) thick.

Sprinkle a handful of mozzarella over the base and season generously with salt, pepper, thyme leaves and chilli flakes, to taste. Add a few dried lemon slices. Repeat with three more pieces of dough to make four little pizzas. Remove the hot baking trays from the oven and use a spatula and your other hand to transfer two pizzas onto each, making sure they are spaced at least 1 cm (½ inch) apart. Bake for 7 minutes or until the edges are browned and crispy (less if you have a proper pizza oven).

Repeat with the remaining ingredients to make another four pizzas and bake as soon as the first batch comes out of the oven. Scatter over the lemon zest and enjoy the first batch while the second batch cools slightly. Slice the pizzette into wedges and serve from a chopping board or serving dish alongside the rest of your aperitivo.

VARIATION

TOMATO AND CHILLI TOPPING:– If you would like to offer two types of pizza, you can make four of the lemon and four with tomato and chilli (another favourite). Cut 200 g (7 oz) datterini cherry tomatoes in half lengthways and then widthways so they are in quarters. Toss them in a small bowl with some fine sea salt, ½ teaspoon dried oregano, a finely chopped red chilli (deseeded if you don't like it too hot) and a few chilli flakes. Spoon some of the mixture over a prepared pizza base, leaving a dough border, and drizzle over some olive oil. Bake in the hot, hot oven for 10 minutes until the crusts are brown (less if you have a proper pizza oven).

DALL'ORTO

FROM THE VEGETABLE PATCH

DALL'ORTO

 I've often wondered why Italy has such a strong food culture. The reason I keep coming back to is quite simple – its produce. Few places boast such perfect conditions for food production, with its Mediterranean climate, volcanic soil and years of careful cultivation. Nowhere is this more evident than on Italy's west coast, the lands that abut the Tyrrhenian. Here, Italy's three great active volcanoes – Etna, Stromboli and Vesuvius – dominate the landscape but also infuse the soil with nutrients: potassium, iron, magnesium and calcium. The remnants of lava and volcanic ash, which spread for miles when an eruption takes place, enhance the earth's fertility long after the event. As a result, produce grown here will have a crisper texture and more intense flavour. Pluck a tomato off a vine and you will taste something quite unlike the homogenous greenhouse-trained fruits we find in supermarkets elsewhere. And that richness extends to everything – the pastures where the buffalo graze to produce mozzarella, and the wheat fields where grain is harvested to make bread and pasta. The vegetables that grow here – glorious tomatoes; gluts of pale, dark green or yellow zucchini; bulbous dark, pale violet or eggshell-coloured aubergines; and enormous red and yellow peppers – make the cuisine universal, but also very different, as each area has its own innovative way of using up these same ingredients, depending on the other materials they have on hand and the cultural influences they have inherited.

The fertility of the soil and temperate climate make growing vegetables an easy task, rather than the uphill battle it can be in colder northern climes. The orto (or vegetable patch) is a beloved and much-practised tradition dating back to Ancient Rome, when it was integrated into the design of all domestic dwellings. In fact, it was believed that the divinities protecting each person's house were specifically watching over the family orto. In the 20th century, home-grown vegetables became vital to sustain communities during the wars, with the fascist regime in Italy decreeing in 1940 that all public gardens and green spaces be turned into allotments; this was later extended to any urban outdoor space, such as balconies or rooftops. Most people I know in Italy have some form of vegetable patch, and talking about vegetables is a favourite past-time. Ask at the market for a kilogram of zucchini and the stallholder will almost certainly ask what you plan

to do with them as this will have a bearing on the ripeness, quality and/or colour of the produce they pick out for you. This information is often volunteered even if the greengrocer doesn't ask, and I am often caught out by my impatient Anglo-Saxon temperament as an elderly customer in front of me goes into elaborate unsolicited detail while I stand there crossly waiting for my turn. Inevitably my spirits lift on hearing what they will do with the vegetables, and this little mental journey is a reminder to slow down and not always be in a rush.

Around our home in Tuscany, the allotment is sometimes even a place of business. When I was a child, whenever my father was trying to get something done – like commissioning a builder or dealing with some matter at the bank – he made a point of finding out where they kept their orto. In the warmer months he would head straight there, knowing they would be in a good mood and more inclined to help than they would be in their hot, stuffy offices. As a result, business agreements were often reached while these officials were training a tomato plant or harvesting zucchini as my sister and I played in the long grass.

This chapter reflects the variety of vegetables available along the Italian coast and a few of the different ways to make the most of them: sometimes tossing through pasta, braising in a little oil, or cooking quickly with beaten eggs to make a gloriously thin and satisfying frittata.

Frittata di zucchine

A VERY THIN ZUCCHINI AND BASIL OMELETTE

I first came across this quick and easy summer dish when I was lunching with friends in a restaurant in southern Tuscany on a baking hot day. We placed our order and happily carried on chatting and sipping chilled wine, getting hungrier by the minute. After nearly an hour, the waiter realised he'd forgotten to put our order through. He disappeared into the kitchen and almost immediately reappeared with a frittata di zucchine to apologise and tide us over. Needless to say, the sweet basil and zucchini encased in egg and cheese was delicious. If you'd like to offer this as a main, allow one per person and serve with salad.

PREPARATION:– 10 minutes
COOKING:– 15 minutes

SERVES 1 AS A MAIN OR 2–3 AS A STARTER

2 organic eggs

sea salt and freshly ground black pepper

25 g (1 oz) unsalted butter

1 tablespoon olive oil

1 zucchini (about 150 g/5½ oz), top removed, sliced into thin discs

handful of basil leaves, roughly torn

20 g (¾ oz) parmesan, finely grated

Crack the eggs into a small bowl, add a generous pinch of salt and a few grinds of pepper and whisk with a fork.

Melt the butter with the olive oil in a wide frying pan over a medium heat. Pick up the pan and swirl the fat around so that it goes up the side of the pan to avoid the egg sticking later. Once it starts to sizzle, add the zucchini and gently toss to ensure it is evenly coated in oil and butter. Leave to cook without stirring for 3–4 minutes. Add the basil and toss, turning all the zucchini slices over to brown the other side. Cook for another 3–4 minutes until the slices are golden on both sides and the basil has wilted.

Make sure the zucchini is evenly spaced in one layer over the base of the pan. Pour over the beaten egg, then gently swirl the pan to allow the egg to evenly coat the zucchini and spread slightly up the side of the pan. Cook without stirring for 2–3 minutes. Once the egg starts to look opaque at the bottom, sprinkle over the grated parmesan, then leave for another minute or so until the bottom is completely cooked, the top is set and the cheese has melted.

Using a spatula, gently ease the frittata onto a serving plate, cheese side up. Top with some freshly ground pepper and serve immediately.

VARIATION:– This frittata is also delicious with datterini cherry tomatoes. Cut a large handful of cherry tomatoes in half lengthways and continue as described above, replacing the zucchini with the tomatoes.

ROAST PEPPERS WITH SALSA VERDE AND BURRATA

Ruby red and canary yellow peppers roasted to the point of collapse, served with mozzarella and a zingy green salsa verde was a staple that my mother would make for friends when I was little. She would put the cooked peppers in plastic bags (not the environmental pariahs in the 1990s that they are today) and leave them to steam off their skins. After painstakingly peeling away the filmy layer she would arrange the flesh on a platter in beautiful alternating colours, spoon over the vivid green sauce and place two bright white balls of mozzarella in the middle. These days instead of plastic bags I pop the hot peppers in a pot with a lid for 20 minutes. The longer you leave them to steam, the easier it is to pull away the skin. It is a little laborious but it makes the flesh much lovelier to eat so I really wouldn't skip this step.

PREPARATION:– 30 minutes, plus standing time
COOKING:– 40 minutes

SERVES 6

3 large peppers, preferably a mixture of red and yellow

2 tablespoons olive oil

3 large balls of burrata or buffalo mozzarella, drained

SALSA VERDE

100 ml (3½ fl oz) extra virgin olive oil

juice of ½ lemon, or to taste

large handful of basil leaves, finely chopped

large handful of flat-leaf parsley leaves, finely chopped

small handful of mint leaves, finely chopped

1 teaspoon brined capers, rinsed and finely chopped

1 garlic clove, crushed

pinch of sea salt, or to taste

Preheat the oven to 180°C (350°F) fan-forced.

Place the whole peppers in a large roasting tin and brush with olive oil. Roast in the oven for 40 minutes until they have collapsed in on themselves and the skins are charred and blistered. Place the blackened peppers in a large saucepan with a tight-fitting lid, cover and leave to steam for at least 20 minutes.

Meanwhile, make your salsa verde. Pour the olive oil and lemon juice into a bowl, then add the remaining ingredients and stir to combine. Taste and adjust the seasoning and acidity as preferred.

When the peppers have finished steaming, remove one from the pan, being careful as it will still be hot. Gently tug the top, which should now come away easily, bringing with it all the seeds and insides. Place in a bowl or kitchen scrap bin. Pull off the charred and filmy skins – the peppers will start to fall apart in your hands as they are very tender, but that's fine. As you finish peeling each piece, arrange it on a serving dish in a concentric circle. This will take 15–20 minutes so pull up a chair and enjoy the process.

Place the burrata balls in the centre of the peppers and spoon over the salsa verde so the red and yellow strips are dotted with the bright green sauce. Serve at room temperature.

Vignarola

SPRING VEGETABLE STEW WITH CROSTINI AND PROSCIUTTO DOLCE

This Roman stew, made all over Lazio, is designed to celebrate the short window in spring when fresh peas and broad beans are available. This is quite an event and happens to coincide with the last artichokes before they disappear for the summer. I have tried a few variations and settled on this minty vegetarian version, alongside crisp crostini drizzled with very good olive oil. For non-vegetarians, I serve slices of voluptuous prosciutto San Daniele – a variety of prosciutto crudo known as 'dolce'. It is sweeter and less lean than prosciutto di Parma, making it the perfect salty companion to the wholesome vignarola.

Preparing the vegetables is a bit of a labour of love. When you're shopping for ingredients, bear in mind that fresh unpodded peas yield about two-fifths of actual shelled peas, and broad beans about one-quarter. Thankfully this recipe does not call for the broad beans to be double-podded, which really is a faff. I like to set myself up at a table to do the shelling, staring into space or listening to the radio as I release these delicious little morsels from their pods; it's very therapeutic and the results well worth it. If you're short of time you can make this dish with jarred artichoke hearts and frozen beans and peas; it won't be quite as delicious, but on the upside it's very quick to throw together (see variation, opposite).

PREPARATION:– 30 minutes, plus cooling time
COOKING:– 50 minutes

SERVES 6

250 g (9 oz) shelled broad beans (about 800 g/1 lb 12 oz in pods)

250 g (9 oz) shelled peas (about 500 g/1 lb 2 oz in pods)

½ lemon

4 small artichokes

1 tablespoon unsalted butter

2 tablespoons olive oil, plus extra for drizzling

1 red onion, diced

4 mint sprigs, leaves picked

sea salt and freshly ground black pepper

100 ml (3½ fl oz) white wine, plus extra if needed

Before you start preparing the vegetables line up two medium bowls and a very large bowl for all the discarded pods. Use your thumb to crack open the seam of the broad bean pods and empty the beans into one of the empty bowls. Remove the stem at the top of each bean.

Repeat with the pea pods, putting the shelled peas in the second medium bowl.

Squeeze the lemon juice into a bowl of cold water and drop in the lemon half. You will put your prepped artichokes in the acidulated water to stop them turning brown. Take an artichoke and tear off the rough outer leaves (the ones that feel rough in your hands, and that your digestive system is clearly not up to). Using a vegetable peeler, peel away the dark green from the stem until you reach a lighter green. Rub the newly exposed tender flesh with the lemon half. Cut the top third off the artichoke, then cut the prepared artichoke into quarters lengthways and remove the hairy 'choke' with a paring knife. Drop the quarters into the lemony water and repeat with the remaining artichokes.

Melt the butter with 1 tablespoon of olive oil in a heavy wide-bottomed frying pan or shallow flameproof casserole dish over medium heat until lightly sizzling. Add the onion, half the mint and a pinch of salt and cook for 4–5 minutes until the

CROSTINI

6 large slices of white sourdough (preferably a little stale), cut 2 cm (¾ inch) thick

olive oil, for drizzling

sea salt

12 very thin slices of prosciutto di San Daniele (about 100 g/3½ oz)

TO SERVE

50 ml (1¾ fl oz) olive oil

handful of roughly chopped mint leaves

onion is soft and translucent. Add the broad beans and artichokes (reserving the soaking water) and stir until they are well coated in the oil and onion. Cook for a couple of minutes, then add two ladlefuls of the lemony water, along with another generous pinch of salt. Reduce the heat, cover and cook for 5 minutes.

Add the peas, white wine, remaining olive oil and the rest of the mint. Partially cover and cook gently for 20 minutes, stirring occasionally and tasting to check the seasoning. Add a little more lemony water and/or wine if it starts to dry out. When all the vegetables are tender, uncover and cook for a further 5 minutes, allowing the liquid to reduce down. Remove from the heat and allow to cool while you make your crostini.

Preheat the oven to 100°C (200°F) fan-forced.

Spread out the bread slices on a large baking tray and bake for 10 minutes, turning over halfway through to make sure the bread is completely dried out. Transfer to a large plate and drizzle with good olive oil. Sprinkle with sea salt and theatrically drape over slices of the prosciutto.

Dress the vignarole with a little olive oil and scatter over the mint. Serve with the crostini alongside.

VARIATION

USING FROZEN OR JARRED VEGETABLES:– You can make this using jarred artichoke hearts and frozen peas and broad beans. Just be aware they will need far less cooking time than fresh. Drain the artichoke and add to the onion mixture with the broad beans. Cook for about 2 minutes, then add 250 ml (8½ fl oz) water, the juice of ½ lemon and the wine. When you've added the peas, simmer uncovered for 10 minutes. Continue with the recipe, checking the seasoning before serving.

GIGLIO AND THE TUSCAN ISLANDS

 Think of Tuscany and the view that springs to mind is rolling hills dotted with cypress trees and swaying fields of corn. It is not craggy islands or hidden beaches with excellent seafood. And yet the Tuscan archipelago, the most northerly point of the Tyrrhenian just off the coast beyond Monte Argentario, offers just that – a cluster of seven islands, each as distinct and surprising as the next.

Elba is the most famous, thanks to Napoleon's period of exile here, and is also the largest and most densely populated. Its soil has yielded iron for millennia, first to the Etruscans, then later becoming a Greek and Roman stronghold. Its original name was Aethana or Aethalia from the Greek 'aithalos' (smoke) because of the thick clouds of smoke coming from the furnaces. When the Greeks moved the mines to the mainland, where it was cheaper, Elba sank into poverty and was successively invaded, including by the British for two years in the late 18th century. Shortly after this it became the home of the emperor Napoleon, who was appointed King of Elba and given this little spot to rule in an attempt to satisfy his grandiose ambitions. It didn't work, and he escaped in 1815. Elba changed hands between the Florentines and Pisans as those two city states vied for supremacy on the mainland and across the Tyrrhenian. A couple of centuries earlier it had been absorbed into the Spanish Empire (1596) and this complicated history is reflected in one of the island's signature dishes, Gurguglione, a Spanish version of Sicilian caponata but with no vinegar, sugar or raisins.

The food of Elba is generally simple and frugal, with an emphasis on fresh herbs. Dishes that were traditionally made at home have migrated to the island's restaurants as they now champion local cuisine. Bonito fish is cooked in various ways: with fresh spring peas (see page 139); stoccaficco, an air-dried cod (different from baccalà, which is salted) is soaked for twenty-four hours and stewed in soups; and the ultimate seaside cucina povera dish, a soup of cavolo nero and anchovies.

Much more glamorous and exciting than Elba to my mind is Giglio, my favourite of them all. It takes just an hour by ferry from the port of Santo Stefano on the Tuscan peninsula of Monte Argentario. The arrival into the jaunty small port is magical, so simple in its beauty with its contrasting pastel-coloured buildings. In this bustling Italian waterfront, the restaurants sit on stilts above the crystal-clear water and fisherman vie for the best spots to moor their small boats. As you leave Porto Santa Stefano, the views open up with the wide expanse of sea to your left and the Tuscan coast to your right. As you approach Giglio a castellated town comes into view, perched on one of the island's highest points. Giglio inhabitants would historically retreat to Castello when the island was being invaded by pirates, which was often. It is the culinary legacy of one such attack that makes me feel very at home on Giglio, as their signature panficato is a variation on the Sienese panforte – a chewy nougaty cake made with nuts, raisins and honey, typical of where I grew up. This came about following the 1544 attack by the pirate Barbarossa, who took many of the islanders captive and slaughtered the rest. Following the massacre, the Medici family decided to repopulate this far-flung outpost of the Duchy of Tuscany with people from Siena. When they arrived they found an abundance of figs and decided to add them to the traditional panforte recipe, along with chocolate, to make the island's now-classic sweet treat.

A more contemporary tragedy brought world fame to this sleepy little island when in 2011 Captain Francesco Schettino steered the *Costa Concordia* cruise ship into rocks facing the port, killing thirty-two people and landing himself a considerable stint in prison. The wreck took seven years to dismantle and the island's largest hotel was rented by the government to house the engineers and divers removing the debris. When the task was complete the hotel was bought by a lovely Roman couple, Flaminia and Matteo, who revamped the dilapidated building into the glorious La Guardia hotel.

Giglio has never been glitzy like Positano or Porto Ercole, though it has hosted some Hollywood royalty. Audrey Hepburn loved to visit and was famed for going on energetic trots up the mountain. Most of the island has remained undeveloped, so Giglio has managed to retain its easy, laid-back charm. This was clear one sunny spring day when Flaminia drove me down a pothole-filled dirt track hugging the side of the mountain with an alarmingly steep drop to the sea on the other side. My vertigo was abated by the beauty of the wildflowers and terraces of vineyards, impressively stepping down in ledges towards the shimmering water far below. When we arrived at our destination it looked like we were in an abandoned field, but Flaminia expertly headed towards a gap in the bushes and we emerged in another vineyard and up to a little white hut beautifully terraced with a modern wooden deck and pergola. We had arrived at Giovanni and Simone Rossi's annual supplier wine tasting, and the setting could not have been more spectacular, sitting in a shady spot among their vineyards overlooking the Tyrrhenian.

Wine was historically the largest export of the island, with even the Duke of Wellington stopping by to restock his ship's supplies. Nowadays there are only a handful of wineries – the Rossi's Fontuccia label among them – who must brave the tricky terrain and island climate to make the local Ansonica wine, an amber-coloured and astringent white wine native to Giglio. Flaminia told me that in the low season (between November and February), islanders take it in turns to host candlelit wine-tasting evenings in their cellars, enjoying simple food and inevitably staggering home very late in the dark and cold.

Visible from the south side of Giglio is the tiny island of Giannutri, which famously houses the ruins of a sumptuous Roman villa, complete with ancient mosaics. Next door is Montecristo, a small conical island which served as the King of Italy's hunting reserve during the 1920s and 1930s. After the King's abdication, the Republic of Italy leased the island to a Milanese family and these days only one custodian and his wife live there. The other three outposts of the archipelago – Pianosa, Gorgona and Capraia – are so remote that they have been used as prisons by the Italian state. At one time they were home to some of Italy's most dangerous criminals and Mafia bosses, but today only Gorgona maintains the tradition. According to Matthew Fort, who made a culinary tour of the island for his 2017 book *Summer in the Islands*, life on Gorgona is rather civilised. As an open-air prison, inmates can keep goats and bees and grow their own vegetables. Prisoners enjoying la dolce vita? Only in Italy.

DALL'ORTO

Caponata eoliana con mozzarella di bufala

CAPONATA WITH BUFFALO MOZZARELLA

This recipe brings together two great culinary traditions by pairing buffalo mozzarella (which is made in Campania, near Naples) with caponata, possibly one of the most emblematic dishes of Sicily and the Aeolian Islands. To me this dish is representative of the islands' remote position in the Tyrrhenian, directly on the historic trading route between Palermo and Naples. Caponata reflects key influences from Sicily's varied cultural past – sweet and sour from the Arabs, and tomatoes from the Spanish. It pairs beautifully with the slightly acidic milky taste of buffalo mozzarella, and is particularly heavenly scooped up with a piece of sourdough (the Italians call the action of scooping up any remaining sauce with bread as doing a 'scarpetta' or little shoe). As one surly Sicilian cook once told me, a traditional caponata takes a long time to make because it involves so much chopping and frying – her version called for each ingredient to be deep-fried separately in batches, so I do see why she found it irksome, though the result was divinely rich and unctuous.

This recipe opts for a less time-consuming method. The aubergine is roasted in the oven to make the dish a little lighter, but feel free to fry it for 5 minutes in a generous splash of vegetable oil if you prefer. I usually use the salted large capers from Salina, soaked in water for 2 hours, although you could also use capers in brine, which don't need any soaking.

PREPARATION:– 15 minutes, plus soaking time
COOKING:– 1 hour 15 minutes

Continues overleaf →

1 large aubergine (about 600 g/1 lb 5 oz), cut into 3 cm (1¼ inch) cubes

100 ml (3½ fl oz) olive oil

sea salt and freshly ground black pepper

100 g (3½ oz) blanched almonds

½ red onion, roughly chopped

2 celery sticks, cut into 2 cm (¾ inch) pieces

100 g (3½ oz) large green olives, pitted and cut into quarters

3 tablespoons salted capers, soaked in water for 2 hours

400 ml (13½ fl oz) tomato passata

2 teaspoons caster sugar

1 tablespoon white wine vinegar

1 tablespoon pine nuts

handful of basil leaves

TO SERVE

olive oil

6 slices of fresh sourdough

flaky sea salt

2 large balls of buffalo mozzarella, cut into quarters

Preheat the oven to 180°C (350°F) fan-forced.

Place the aubergine on a baking tray, toss with 2 tablespoons of olive oil and a pinch of salt and roast for 20 minutes.

Meanwhile, spread out the almonds on a separate baking tray and toast in the oven for about 5 minutes, until they darken and start to smell nutty. Remove from the oven, set aside to cool, then roughly chop.

Pour 2 tablespoons of olive oil into a wide frying pan and heat over a medium heat. Add the onion, celery and a pinch of salt and gently fry, stirring occasionally, for 3 minutes or until translucent. Add the olives, capers and remaining olive oil and stir until well combined and everything is lightly coated with oil. Measure out the tomato passata and pour into the pan. Half-fill the measuring jug with water, swish it around to pick up any remaining passata and pour the tomatoey water into the pan, giving everything a good stir. Cook for 15 minutes. Add the roasted aubergine, sugar and a generous pinch of salt, then cover and cook over a very low heat for 25–30 minutes.

Remove the caponata from the heat and stir through the vinegar, pine nuts, chopped almonds and basil. Allow to cool to room temperature. The longer you leave the caponata the more delicious it will be as the flavours will have melded together. If you are eating it the next day, store it in the fridge overnight, then take out least an hour before serving so it comes back to room temperature.

When you're ready to serve, drizzle olive oil liberally over the bread and sprinkle with flaky salt. Serve with the caponata and mozzarella.

MAURIZIA'S POTATO, OLIVE AND CAPER SALAD

Maurizia is a fifth-generation caper farmer on the island of Salina. Her farm sits above the beautiful bay of Pollara on the northwest coast, best known as the beach where the postman Enzo has his philosophical conversations with the exiled poet Pablo Neruda in the film *Il Postino*. Maurizia ships her capers and caper-based products all over the world, and also offers tastings at the farm, which I heartily recommend. We feasted on small capers dressed in oil, oregano and garlic; medium capers in agrodolce (with vinegar and sweet Malvasia wine); garlic caper paté; chilli, caper and almond paste on toast; sweet caper paste made with lots of sugar and Malvasia, served with a good strong cheese; and candied capers on ricotta-laden bread – the tiny black capers all sticky, salty and treacly. One of the many special products that Maurizia makes is a granella di capperi (dessicated capers blitzed in a food processor). A sprinkle over salads, pasta or vegetables just before serving adds a wonderful aromatic texture.

One dish that has stayed with me from that day is Maurizia's insalata eoliana, a delicious potato and caper salad, the recipe for which she kindly shares here. The key to the perfect texture is to cook the potatoes and soak the capers well in advance, so you can do these steps ahead of time and forget about them until you want to assemble the salad.

PREPARATION:– 15 minutes, plus soaking and standing time
COOKING:– 20 minutes

DELICIOUS WITH:– This is a wonderful vegetarian main on its own or as part of a wider spread of Crostini with ricotta, lemon and crunchy sage; Garlicky grilled tomatoes, and Beef carpaccio with zucchini, rocket and pecorino (pages 55, 176 and 159).

8 waxy potatoes (about 1 kg/
2 lb 3 oz), peeled and left whole

60 g (2 oz) large salted capers
(or capers in brine)

½ red onion, sliced into
half moons

16 cherry tomatoes, cut into
quarters lengthways

1 large cucumber, peeled and
sliced into pieces a similar size
to the tomatoes

handful of good-quality
olives (black or green),
cut in half and pitted

handful of basil leaves,
roughly torn if large

½ teaspoon dried oregano

sea salt

4 tablespoons good-quality
olive oil

1 tablespoon granella di capperi
from Sapori Eoliane (optional)

Cook the potatoes in a large saucepan of salted boiling water for about 20 minutes until you can easily pierce them with a fork. Drain. For the best textural result, do this 4–5 hours before assembling the salad to allow the potatoes to cool completely.

Meanwhile, if you are using salted capers, rinse them in room-temperature water and leave to soak for at least 2 hours, preferably 6 hours. Use plenty of water so they are fully submerged. Change the water four times to be sure you have washed all the salt off.

About 20 minutes before you assemble the salad, soak the onion in a bowl of cold water to mellow the flavour.

Cut the potatoes into bite-sized chunks and arrange on a large serving dish. Add the drained capers – Maurizia recommends giving them a squeeze with your hands first to make sure you've drained all the water. Add the onion, tomatoes, cucumber, olives, basil and oregano, followed by a good pinch of salt and a generous drizzle of olive oil. Toss well, then let the salad sit for an hour if possible to allow the flavours to come together and amalgamate.

If you have any, sprinkle over a tablespoon of granella di capperi just before serving to add a bit of crunch.

Sformato di melanzane

BAKED AUBERGINE AND RICOTTA SFORMATO WITH TOMATO SAUCE

I was served this dish in a restaurant in Cefalù and it immediately became a firm favourite. It combines the flavours of a classic melanzana parmigiana but in a sformato – a kind of cross between a souffle and a savoury flan, made with ricotta, eggs and often a vegetable puree. I've had them with asparagus, spinach and broad beans, usually smothered in a rich bechamel or tomato sauce. You can make individual portions in a muffin tin and spoon over the tomato sauce when plating up, but I usually make a large one in a ring mould as I like the drama of the sauce running from the central well as you cut into it. If you don't have a ring mould, you can use any non-stick container (such as a 20 cm/8 inch cake tin), then simply pour the tomato sauce over the top.

PREPARATION:– 20 minutes, plus cooling time
COOKING:– 50 minutes

2 large aubergines
(about 900 g/2 lb)

3 tablespoons olive oil

2 garlic cloves, peeled
and lightly squashed with
the edge of a knife

1 whole dried red chilli

a few mint leaves,
finely chopped

sea salt and freshly ground
black pepper

250 g (9 oz) ricotta, drained

60 g (2 oz) parmesan,
plus extra to coat the ring
mould and to serve

2 large organic eggs

a little freshly grated nutmeg

1 tablespoon '00' flour

butter, to grease the tin

2–4 tablespoons fine
breadcrumbs

TOMATO SAUCE

2 tablespoons olive oil

1 garlic clove, unpeeled,
lightly squashed with the
edge of a knife

1 large handful of basil leaves,
plus extra to serve

sea salt

500 ml (17 fl oz) tomato passata

Cut the tops off the aubergines and use a potato peeler to peel away the skin. Slice into 2 cm (¾ inch) cubes, keeping the size consistent so they cook evenly.

Heat 2 tablespoons of the olive oil, the garlic cloves and whole chilli in a wide frying pan with a lid over a medium heat. Leave to infuse for about 3 minutes, then remove and discard the garlic and chilli. Add the aubergine and mint and season with a generous pinch of salt and a few grinds of pepper. Cook, stirring, for 2–3 minutes until the aubergine takes on a little colour and pour over the remaining olive oil.

Reduce the heat to low and cook, covered, for 10–12 minutes, stirring occasionally. The aubergine is cooked when it has all slumped and looks translucent. Transfer to a large mixing bowl and blitz to a puree using a handheld blender. Set aside to cool at room temperature for at least 10 minutes or up to 2 days in the fridge.

Preheat the oven to 180°C (350°F) fan-forced.

Add the ricotta, parmesan, eggs and nutmeg to the cooled aubergine and season with a generous pinch of salt and some more pepper. Mix with a spoon or whisk until everything is fully amalgamated. Add the flour and mix again until you have a smooth batter.

Butter a 20 cm (8 inch) savarin ring mould, then sprinkle with the breadcrumbs and a little parmesan, tilting the mould to ensure the sides and base are evenly coated. Pour the batter into the mould, levelling it out with the back of a spoon. Bake for 30 minutes or until a cake tester comes out clean(ish).

Meanwhile, make the tomato sauce. Gently warm the olive oil, garlic clove and basil in a frying pan over a low heat for 2–3 minutes. Add a pinch of salt, followed by the passata, then leave to bubble away for 15 minutes, stirring occasionally and tasting as you go. Remove from the heat and set aside. Fish out the garlic clove and discard.

Remove the baked ricotta from the oven and allow to cool for 15 minutes.

Place a serving plate over the mould and invert the baked ricotta onto the plate. Fill the centre with the tomato sauce. If any excess liquid gathers at the base of the baked ricotta, dab it with paper towel. Sprinkle with extra grated parmesan and arrange some basil leaves on top for decoration. The sformato is delicious hot from the oven, or at room temperature on a hot summer's day.

VARIATIONS

MOZZARELLA:– If I'm serving the sformato hot from the oven, I often add a handful of diced fior di latte mozzarella to the ring mould as a melted cheese surprise. Drain a large ball of mozzarella, cut it in half and dice into 1 cm (½ inch) cubes. Pour half the sformato mixture into the ring mould and scatter the diced mozzarella around the ring. Pour over the rest of the sformato mixture and bake as described above, leaving time to rest for 15 minutes.

TOMATO SALAD:– This is also delicious with a fresh tomato salad instead of tomato sauce. While the sformato is in the oven, cut 300 g (10½ oz) cherry tomatoes into quarters and place in a bowl. Add a handful of finely chopped basil, ½ teaspoon fine sea salt and 2 tablespoons olive oil, then leave for at least 15 minutes for the flavours to come together. Once you have unmoulded the sformato, spoon the tomato salad into the centre, or on top if you haven't used a ring mould.

L'acquacotta di Viviana

VIVIANA'S ACQUACOTTA

Acquacotta is a thick Tuscan soup typical of Maremma. It originated on Monte Amiata, the once-volcanic mountain that dominates southern Tuscany. Known as the 'dish of nomads', it was invented by poor farmers who lived in the mountains but had to come down to the coast to fish or work in the fields. They would bring with them a loaf of stale bread, a braid of onions and, if they could afford it, pancetta, pecorino cheese and a few eggs. The ingredients would vary depending on the seasons and how poor they were – the most frugal version was simply cabbage stewed in water. Today there are as many recipes for acquacotta as there are for a classic tomato sauce, but in essence it is a vegetable soup cooked for hours to get the best flavour out of the most basic ingredients: onion, celery, tomato and egg. The original acquacotta ('cooked water') had no egg as this came much later, but some say the farmers would fry an egg in a pan and then use the same pan to make the acquacotta so it would soak up the fat and flavour. Nowadays the eggs are generally poached in the soup.

Viviana is a wonderful cook from Capalbio. Her acquacotta is rich, sweet and hearty, perfect for filling the bellies of hungry agricultural workers. The secret is very gentle, slow cooking as well as thoroughly removing the outer stringy bits from the celery, which sounds like a faff but is super quick and easy. So don't be put off by how long this recipe takes; it is very easy to make and it is even better the next day. It is also very tasty without the parmesan and egg if you follow a vegan diet.

PREPARATION:– 20 minutes
COOKING:– 3 hours

500 g (1 lb 2 oz) celery,
woody ends removed

100 ml (3½ fl oz) olive oil

sea salt

250 ml (8½ fl oz) dry white wine

4 large white onions,
finely chopped

800 g (1 lb 12 oz) tin peeled
plum tomatoes

4 slices stale bread (or dried
crostini; see page 55)

120 g (4½ oz) finely grated
pecorino or parmesan

4 large organic eggs

Using a vegetable peeler, lightly peel the outer ribs of each celery stick to get rid of the stringy bits, then slice them into 1 cm (½ inch) chunks. If there are any celery leaves, roughly chop and add them as well.

Pour half the olive oil into a large saucepan, add the celery and a pinch of salt and gently sweat over a medium heat for 10 minutes, stirring occasionally. Add the wine and another pinch of salt and stir well, then cover and simmer over a low heat for 40 minutes, checking and stirring occasionally. Add a tablespoon or two of water and another drizzle of olive oil if the celery looks like it's drying out.

Add the onion and another pinch of salt and stir until well combined. Cook for 30 minutes, stirring occasionally, until the vegetables are well and truly tender.

Add the tomatoes, breaking them up with the end of the wooden spoon. Half-fill the empty tin with water and swish it around to pick up any remaining tomato and pour the tomatoey water into the pan. Add another 300 ml (10 fl oz) water, along with the rest of the olive oil and a pinch more salt, and leave the acquacotta to cook gently over a low heat for at least 1 hour and up to 1 hour 30 minutes. Keep an eye on it and stir and taste occasionally; if it looks like it's reducing too much, add another 100 ml (3½ fl oz) water. When it's ready, the flavour should be an intense amalgam of celery, onion and tomato, with enough liquid to poach the eggs in.

At this point you can cover and store the soup in the fridge for up to 3 days. It's delicious the next day, once the flavours have had time to mingle and develop.

When you're ready to serve, place a slice of bread, cut into quarters, in the bottom of four shallow bowls and evenly sprinkle with the grated cheese.

Add three or four ladlefuls of the acquacotta to a deep, wide frying pan and heat over a medium until the liquid starts bubbling. Crack in the eggs, making sure they are well spaced apart, then reduce the heat, cover and gently poach for 4–5 minutes. When the egg whites are opaque but the yolks are still runny, switch off the heat, uncover and set aside.

Meanwhile, heat the main pot of acquacotta. It should be piping hot when served.

Ladle some of the hot acquacotta over the bread and parmesan in each bowl, making sure each portion has plenty of onion and celery and some of the intense red liquid. Using a tablespoon, gently lift a poached egg into each bowl to perch on top. Sprinkle over some salt and serve immediately.

CALAMARATA PASTA WITH AUBERGINE, OLIVES, PECORINO ROMANO AND ALMONDS

Sperlonga is a pretty clifftop town on Lazio's southern coast approaching the border with Campania. Its unique elevated position on the Ulysses Riviera means that it has glorious views towards Monte Circeo in the north and Gaeta in the south. I once stopped there at Bar Il Trani, where I had a pasta dish that contained aubergine but no tomato, its usual stablemate. Instead, the dish featured one of Lazio's best-known exports – pecorino romano – as well as the Latina coast's most covetable produce, Gaeta olives. The dish stayed with me, and this is my interpretation of how they might have made it. It is not 'officially' the pasta of Sperlonga, but I have named it so as that is where I ate it. The original was served with paccheri – large, smooth tubes of pasta from Naples. I find them a little unwieldy so have replaced them with pasta calamarata, which are also from Naples. It's really important with this recipe to get proper olives and not the plain pitted ones in tins.

PREPARATION:– 10 minutes
COOKING:– 35 minutes

SERVES 6

1 large aubergine
(about 600 g/1 lb 5 oz)

100 g (3½ oz) flaked almonds

75 ml (2½ fl oz) olive oil,
plus extra to serve

1 garlic clove, unpeeled,
lightly squashed with the
edge of a knife

sea salt and freshly ground
black pepper

80 g (2¾ oz) Gaeta or Kalamata
olives, cut in half lengthways
and pitted

150 ml (5 fl oz) white wine
(anything you have knocking
around in the fridge will do)

500 g (1 lb 2 oz) pasta
calamarata (paccheri or
rigatoni are also fine)

120 g (4½ oz) pecorino romano,
finely grated, plus extra,
coarsely grated, to serve

grated zest of 1 lemon

Remove and discard the top of the aubergine and trim about 5 mm (¼ inch) from the bottom. Slice into 1 cm (½ inch) thick discs and cut into quarters leaving triangular wedges.

In a large frying pan with a tight-fitting lid, toast the flaked almonds over a medium heat for about 3 minutes, tossing often so that they get a little colour and begin to smell nutty but don't burn. Transfer to a bowl and set aside.

Heat 50 ml (1¾ fl oz) of olive oil, the garlic clove and a pinch of salt in the frying pan over a low heat for 2–3 minutes until the garlic gently sizzles and infuses the olive oil. Turn the garlic clove over and add the aubergine, along with a generous pinch of salt and a grind of pepper, tossing well to make sure the aubergine soaks up a bit of oil. Increase the heat to medium–high and leave to cook and get a little colour for 10 minutes, tossing halfway through to ensure the aubergine cooks evenly.

Fish out and discard the garlic clove. Add the olives, wine, remaining olive oil and a pinch of salt, then cover and cook for another 15 minutes.

Meanwhile, bring a large saucepan of salted water to the boil. Add the pasta, give it a good stir so that it doesn't stick together, and cook until al dente (check the packet instructions). Halfway through the cooking time add a ladleful of the starchy pasta water to the aubergine, then leave to bubble away uncovered.

Drain the pasta, reserving a mug of the cooking water in case it's needed to loosen the sauce. Toss the pasta through the aubergine sauce with an extra glug of olive oil.

Toss through the finely grated pecorino, along with 2–3 tablespoons of the pasta water to help it amalgamate with the sauce. Add the almond flakes, half the lemon zest, and a little more salt and pepper. Spoon into bowls and finish with coarsely grated pecorino and the remaining lemon zest.

I 'miei' spaghetti al Nerano

'MY' SPAGHETTI WITH ZUCCHINI AND BASIL

This recipe was inspired by the now-famous spaghetti al Nerano of Ristorante Lo Scoglio (see page 162). It has been one of my favourite dishes ever since I first tried it there years ago, and lots of the seaside restaurants in Marina del Cantone and in nearby Nerano have their own versions too. One reason the original recipe from Lo Scoglio is so indulgent is because they use a variety of cheeses and the zucchini is deep-fried before the sauce is cooked, making it creamy and meaty at the same time. This is great if you are ordering it in a restaurant but a faff to make at home so I have devised a method that gently shallow-fries it instead, using both sliced and grated zucchini. The process is much quicker and results in a lovely meaty texture without needing a deep-fryer.

PREPARATION:– 15 minutes
COOKING:– 35 minutes

SERVES 6

1 kg (2 lb 3 oz) zucchini

olive oil, for pan-frying and to serve

4 garlic cloves, crushed

½ teaspoon chilli flakes

1 large bunch of basil, leaves picked and roughly torn

sea salt and freshly ground black pepper

600 g (1 lb 5 oz) spaghetti or linguine

150 g (5½ oz) parmesan, finely grated, plus extra to serve

Chop the tops and bottoms off the zucchini and separate into two equal piles. Cut one pile into rounds about 2 mm (¹⁄₁₆ inch) thick. Grate the rest of the zucchini using the large holes of a box grater (if you don't have one, cut into fine matchsticks).

Meanwhile, heat 4 tablespoons of olive oil in a wide frying pan over a medium heat and gently fry the garlic and chilli for a couple of minutes. Once the garlic starts sizzling, add the zucchini discs and toss with the oil and garlic, making sure they are all well coated. Leave the zucchini to fry for 5 minutes before turning to cook on the other side for a further 10 minutes, tossing occasionally. You want the discs to brown. Add the grated zucchini, basil (reserving a little for garnish), another 2 tablespoons of olive oil and a generous pinch of salt and pepper. Allow to cook for a further 5 minutes, then pour in half a glass of water (about 150 ml/5 fl oz). Reduce the heat and leave to cook gently while you prepare the pasta.

Bring a large saucepan of salted water to the boil. Add the pasta, give it a good stir so that it doesn't stick together, and cook until al dente (about 9 minutes, but check the packet instructions). Halfway through the pasta cooking time, add a couple of ladlefuls of the starchy pasta water to the zucchini mixture; increase the heat slightly to allow the water to amalgamate into the sauce. Stir in the grated parmesan and another half ladle of pasta water.

Drain the pasta (reserving a mugful of the cooking water in case you need it), then add to the zucchini sauce with a drizzle of olive oil and toss to combine. Top with extra parmesan, a few grinds of pepper and the reserved basil. Serve immediately.

LINGUINE WITH TOMATOES AND CAPERS

This quick, delicious and cheap dish really sums up what is so great about Italian, or in this instance, Aeolian cooking. A good sauce doesn't have to be complicated or lengthy, and you certainly don't have to rely on expensive ingredients. I usually make this pasta when I'm short on time but want something that packs a punch flavour-wise. It is elevated by the floral saltiness of the capers, which immediately transport me to the southern parts of the Tyrrhenian. The type of tomato I use depends on the season. If it's summer and I have cherry tomatoes I will use those, and the sauce only takes as long as the pasta to cook. If not, tinned are just as good and perhaps a bit cosier in the colder months. Ultimately, the only difference is that the sauce will take longer to cook.

PREPARATION:– 10 minutes, plus soaking time
COOKING:– 45 minutes (20 minutes if using fresh tomatoes)

SERVES 5

100 g (3½ oz) salted or brined capers

75 ml (2½ fl oz) olive oil

1 white onion, finely chopped

sea salt

3 garlic cloves, crushed

1 small red chilli, deseeded and finely chopped

500 g (1 lb 2 oz) cherry tomatoes, cut into quarters, or 1 x 400 g (14 oz) tin peeled plum tomatoes

500 g (1 lb 2 oz) linguine or spaghetti

finely grated parmesan, to serve

If you are using salted capers, soak them for about 2 hours, changing the water three times. If you don't have time, use brined capers.

Pour half the olive oil into a frying pan wide enough to hold all the linguine and heat over a medium heat for 30 seconds or so. Add the onion and a pinch of salt and gently fry for 2 minutes. Stir in the garlic and cook for 3–5 minutes until the onion is translucent. Add the capers and chilli and cook for a further 5 minutes.

Add the fresh tomatoes and a pinch of salt and give it a good stir. Simmer for the same time it takes to cook the pasta (about 10 minutes). If you are using tinned, half-fill the empty tin with water, swish it around to pick up any remaining tomato and add the tomatoey water to the pan. Simmer for 30 minutes.

While the sauce is bubbling away, bring a large saucepan of salted water to the boil. Add the pasta, give it a good stir so that it doesn't stick together, and cook until al dente (about 9 minutes, but check the packet instructions). Halfway through the cooking time, add a ladleful of the pasta cooking water to the sauce and increase the heat to high. Scoop out a mugful of the pasta water in case it's needed.

Drain the pasta and toss through the sauce, along with the rest of the olive oil. Add a little of the reserved cooking water if you need to loosen the sauce. Top with finely grated parmesan and serve immediately.

THE SOUTHERN LAZIO COAST

Considering the region is home to Italy's capital, Lazio and its southern coast are amazingly unpolished. Roads are rough and strewn with potholes, prickly pear cacti run rampant along the side of the road, and the sight of locals selling produce out of the back of a battered car truly announces that you have arrived in 'The South'.

This is the land of the Pontine marshes, written about by Livy, Plutarch and Pliny the Elder, where the landscape is very flat but fertile. Today it is dominated by hothouses filled with peonies, 'contadini' (farmers) tending to their plots, and agricultural workers commuting by bicycle on the long straight Roman roads. The only tall landmarks are huge Corsican pine trees. Ancient and modern sit fading side by side, with Roman temples crumbling alongside towns built by Mussolini, some of which had to be rebuilt in the 1950s and 1960s having been decimated during the World War II. Despite the bounty the soil produces, this part of Lazio feels anything but rich.

The region had its heyday in ancient times when it served as the coastal getaway of emperors. The town of Anzio, believed to have been built by Anteias, son of Odysseus and Circe, and now synonymous with the Anglo-American push that helped end the war with Germany, was once one of the most important ports in Ancient Rome. It was built by the emperor Nero who encouraged wealthy Roman families to move there. The decline of the Roman empire saw with it the decline of Anzio. It was revitalised in the 18th century by Pope Innocenzo XII, but was later destroyed in World War II. Nowadays, Anzio has been rebuilt and serves as a coastal summer getaway for Roman families.

A bit further south is the fascist town of Sabaudia, which like Maremma in Tuscany was made up of uninhabitable marshland until the 20th century when Mussolini ordered that the marshes be drained, employing 50,000 members of the 'Opera Nazionale di Combattenti' a charity designed to provide work for veterans from World War I. Draining the marshes was not an original idea, as it had first been suggested by Leonardo Da Vinci. Once the land was ready, Mussolini staged a national competition in 1933 to determine who would design the new town of Sabaudia, which was won by four rationalist architects. Sabaudia was built in less than a year and inaugurated by Italy's King Vittorio Emanuele and Queen Elena of Montenegro, who was also part of the House of Savaoia which is apparently where the name Sabaudia comes from.

Elsewhere along the coast, place names are inspired by the classics, sometimes comically so – to get to Penelope's Lido you head down Via Anchise (father of Aeneas), but not down Via del Centauro, or Via Claudia Augusta, and so on. One restaurant is called 'Aeneas's Landing', a reference to Book IV of Virgil's *Aeneid* in which Aeneas lands in Lazio on his quest to find a site to build a new Troy, which will eventually be Rome. The mountain promontory of Monte Circeo takes its name from the half sorceress, half goddess Circe and is said to be her mythical island home of Aeaea where she lived among lions and other wild animals. As it would have been surrounded by marshes it probably did look like an island at one time. Nowadays it's a popular trekking spot, with many a walk leading to the ruins of a Roman temple dedicated to Circe. The inhabitants of San Felice di Circeo, a town on the mountain slopes, are rightly proud of the history of their home, and one local told me that San Felice is a small place with an important heritage. In 2011 Neolithic remains were found in the Grotta delle Capre (Cave of the Goats) and when I mention to her that we plan to visit Sabaudia, she scoffs and says, 'well, it's not ancient'.

South from Monte Circeo, on the other side of the bay, sits the charming town of Terracina. At the top of its mountain is one of Italy's best preserved Roman temples, Il Tempio di Anxur or Jupiter's Temple. In the town there are some amazing Roman ruins and you can walk along the Appian Way, the first and most famous of the ancient Roman roads. There is also a pretty medieval church, with a hundred-year-old ice-cream shop next door, perfect for sitting and eating pistachio ice-cream sandwiched in a fluffy brioche bun – one of my favourite Sicilian exports to the Italian mainland. The lady I speak to from San Felice tells me of an old enmity between her town and Terracina, joking that the only good thing about Terracina is that on a clear day you can see Monte Circeo from the Temple of Anxur.

Culinarily-speaking, southern Lazio is very much a reflection of its geographical position – halfway between Tuscany and Campania. I'm struck by the austere cucina povera puddings such as ciambelline al vino rosso – dry biscuits made with red wine similar to what you might get in Tuscany, especially on the island of Giglio. But they also have that abundance of produce found further south, such as incredible mozzarella like you find in Campania, as the soil is equally fertile and perfect for rearing buffalo. The mozzarella from here and neighbouring Campania is not like the pasteurised exported stuff we are used to in foreign supermarkets, or even further north within Italy. It is more acidic, sour and tangy from the volcanic soil on which the buffalo graze, with just the right sort of rubbery 'squeak' as you eat it. It's so good it doesn't need dressing in olive oil or salt.

Even as we passed a service station on the side of the road towards Gaeta, my eye was caught by a sign shouting 'MOZZARELLA' and I was thrilled to find that there was the most incredible deli serving simple and fabulous mozzarella sandwiches. Clearly a trucker hotspot, as I ordered our mid-morning snack an enormous lorry pulled over and out hopped an exhausted-looking trucker. The ladies behind the counter didn't even need to ask for his order, handing him a mozzarella sandwich and an open bottle of beer. Holding his bounty he hopped back into the van and trundled off, hopefully sipping on a non-alcoholic beer, though I suspect not.

The simplicity of the perfect mozzarella purveyors is everywhere in Southern Lazio. In San Felice di Circeo there is a wonderful farmer's shop called Caseificio Montecirceo. At the back of the shop are barns filled with buffalo, milked each morning to make a daily quota of every kind of mozzarella imaginable: huge ivory-coloured balls, tiny bite-sized bocconcini, ones which were smoked to eat as a fabulous aperitivo, and delicate ricotta made from the whey. As you stand at the counter you immediately become hungry. One man walked in and asked for one kilogram of bocconcini to have that evening with his family, which sounds like my kind of family supper.

Olives are also important here. Gaeta is the olive-growing capital and it's worth buying Gaeta olives if you see them as they have a particularly rich, intense flavour and firm texture. At the Caseificio they sell them from barrels, ones dried in the oven, plain or seasoned with chilli flakes and oregano to eat with a drink before dinner. You can also buy plain olives for cooking, tossed through pasta such as Calamarata pasta with aubergine, olives, pecorino romano and almonds (page 92) or to be eaten with fish, like Whole sea bream cooked 'in parcels' with lemon, thyme and olives (page 140).

Rightly, there is a lot of pride in this region for what they produce. I once stopped at a bar on a roundabout on the road to Sperlonga from Monte and was hailed by a man selling trays of glorious fruit from the back of his small van. He introduced himself as Franco and proceeded to show off his apples, cherries

(Lazio is famed for its cherries), melons (which he said were the best in Lazio), lemons and fizzy red wine that he made in his garage, which was slightly less of a hit with us than his fresh produce. He seemed self-conscious that the cherries weren't at their best. And when we said we didn't want any he kept repeating, 'I know I know, it's a bit early, they aren't the best these ones.' We bought a couple of things and he gave us a bag of apples and oranges from his garden, plus the bottle of red wine that he'd opened for us to try. As we sat in the bar and had a coffee, I overheard him speaking to the owner – 'Did you make a killing, Franco?', 'Not really, the cherries weren't the best.'

Rigatoni al fuoco

RIGATONI WITH FIERY ROAST TOMATOES AND RICOTTA

This pasta is inspired by the volcanic island of Stromboli in the Aeolian Islands and its fiery unpredictable nature. Stromboli is the most active volcano in Europe and gently bubbles away most evenings. You can hike up to the crater to watch the lava flow, and on a clear day see its gentle eruptions from Salina. I love this dish as it delivers on flavour and deliciousness with minimal effort. All that's required is putting a dish of tomatoes in the oven, followed by the ricotta, cooking the pasta and uniting the two in the baking dish. I like to think of it as an ode to Stromboli through spice and domed ricotta.

PREPARATION:– 10 minutes
COOKING:– 30 minutes

SERVES 5

600 g (1 lb 5 oz) cherry tomatoes, cut into quarters

1 small red chilli, deseeded and finely chopped

¼ teaspoon chilli flakes

75 ml (2½ fl oz) olive oil

sea salt

250 g (9 oz) ricotta, drained

500 g (1 lb 2 oz) rigatoni

75 g (2¾ oz) parmesan, finely grated

handful of basil leaves

Preheat the oven to 180°C (350°F) fan-forced.

Put the cherry tomatoes in a large baking dish (I use one attractive enough to serve from). Add the chopped chilli, chilli flakes, half the olive oil and a couple of generous pinches of salt and toss to combine. Roast for 15 minutes.

Remove the tomatoes from the oven – by now they should have started to steam and collapse. Use a spoon to make a space in the centre and nestle the ricotta into the mixture, wide base downwards so that it looks like a little volcano. Spoon some of the cooking juices over the ricotta, along with another drizzle of olive oil and a pinch of salt. Return to the oven and roast for another 15 minutes.

Meanwhile, bring a large saucepan of salted water to the boil. Add the rigatoni, give it a good stir so that it doesn't stick together, and cook until al dente (about 12–13 minutes, but check the packet instructions). Drain, reserving half a mugful of the pasta water in case it's needed.

Remove the tomatoes and ricotta from the oven. Add the drained rigatoni, parmesan, basil and remaining olive oil and gently toss to combine, with a splash of pasta water if needed. Take the dish to the table and serve immediately.

FUSILLI WITH PISTACHIO PESTO AND LEMON ZEST

I first had pistachio pesto at my dear friend Anita's hotel, the Principe di Salina, on the island of Salina, and this is an interpretation I made as soon as I got home and was longing to be back there. Anita's mother, Silvana, a cardiovascular surgeon turned chef, does all the cooking and makes a fabulous version with fusilli lunghi – tight long coils of pasta that scoop up the pesto perfectly and are a joy to eat. A pesto made with pistachios has a more subtle flavour than the traditional Genovese pesto with pine nuts, but that is what makes this dish so delicious and special. Because you don't want to mask the subtle flavour of the pistachios there is far less garlic and – more importantly – basil than in a regular pesto, so if you want to obtain a vibrant green colour it's necessary to skin the pistachios first. I used to do this, but I don't any more as I actually prefer the texture of bone-dry pistachios and find the pesto is colourful enough without the hassle of removing the skins.

PREPARATION:– 15 minutes, plus standing time
COOKING:– 10 minutes

SERVES 5

500 g (1 lb 2 oz) fusilli (or if you can find them, fusilli lunghi)

PISTACHIO PESTO

300 g (10½ oz) pistachios

50 g (1¾ oz) basil leaves

½ garlic clove

150 ml (5 fl oz) olive oil, plus extra for drizzling

sea salt

grated zest of 1 lemon

juice of ½ lemon

75 g (2¾ oz) parmesan, finely grated, plus extra to serve

To make the pesto, roughly chop half the pistachios in a food processor, making sure they retain some texture. Set aside in a bowl. Add the rest of the pistachios to the processor, along with the basil, garlic, olive oil, salt, lemon zest and juice, and blitz until smooth. Add to the roughly chopped pistachios. Stir in the parmesan and an extra drizzle of olive oil, then leave to infuse for 30 minutes. (If you omit the parmesan you can freeze the pesto, then add it to the thawed pesto before serving.)

Bring a large saucepan of salted water to the boil. Add the pasta and give it a good stir so that it doesn't stick together, then cook until al dente (about 9 minutes, but check the packet instructions). Towards the end of the cooking time, scoop out a mugful of the starchy pasta water in case it's needed.

Drain the pasta and toss in a serving dish with the pesto and a little of the pasta water to bring it together. Finish with a final drizzle of olive oil, top with extra parmesan and serve immediately.

VARIATION

WITH PANCETTA:– To add a touch of salty protein to the pasta, roughly chop or dice 100 g (3½ oz) streaky pancetta. Fry in a small frying pan until crispy, then drain on a plate lined with paper towel and set aside. Sprinkle over the pasta at the last possible moment.

Lasagne con zucchine, menta e besciamella

ZUCCHINI, MINT AND BECHAMEL LASAGNE

This recipe is based on a meal I once had at Capofaro, a wonderful hotel on the island of Salina. The hotel is made up of lots of little cottages dispersed among the property's vineyards, which produce some very fine island wines under the umbrella of the Tasca family, who in turn make fabulous wines throughout Sicily. The restaurant is under the stewardship of chef Gabriele Camiolo, and his ravioli with zucchini, ricotta and mint were a revelation to me: the filling is fresh and light, particularly when encased in gossamer-thin sheets of homemade pasta. I immediately went home and tried to recreate it and, while I love ravioli, I am often cooking for a crowd and simply don't have time to lovingly cut, shape and parcel large quantities of pasta. Instead, I came up with this one-tray baked version in the form of lasagne. If you don't have the time or inclination to make bechamel you can use ricotta instead, which is both quicker and a little lighter. I like both versions so have included a variation with the ricotta (right).

PREPARATION:– 30 minutes, plus standing time
COOKING:– 1 hour 25 minutes

SERVES 8

4 tablespoons olive oil

2 garlic cloves, peeled and lightly squashed with the side of a knife

1.2 kg (2 lb 10 oz) zucchini, sliced into thin discs

sea salt and freshly ground black pepper

handful of mint leaves, roughly chopped

grated zest of 1 lemon

about 350 g (12½ oz) lasagne sheets, preferably fresh, but dried will work too

50 g (1¾ oz) parmesan, finely grated

Heat 2 tablespoons of olive oil and 1 garlic clove in a wide frying pan over a medium heat for 2 minutes or so, allowing the flavour to infuse the oil as it comes up to temperature. When the garlic starts to sizzle, add half the zucchini and a grind of pepper. (Don't add any salt just yet or the zucchini will release liquid and won't brown.) Toss the zucchini to coat in the oil and gently cook for 5 minutes – you want some of the zucchini to brown and some to almost slump, so don't worry if it doesn't all cook evenly. Remove to a bowl and repeat with the remaining olive oil, garlic and zucchini, cooking for 5 minutes. Return all the zucchini to the pan, add the mint and cook for another 10 minutes, tossing often.

Add the lemon zest, 100 ml (3½ fl oz) water and a couple of generous pinches of salt to the zucchini mixture, then reduce the heat and cook for another 10–15 minutes, stirring occasionally, until it reaches a thick sauce consistency. Remove from the heat, fish out and discard the garlic cloves and set aside.

Meanwhile, bring a large saucepan of salted water to the boil and fill a large bowl with cold water. Lay a clean tea towel on a flat surface.

Working in batches if necessary, add the lasagne sheets to the boiling water, making sure the pan isn't too crowded. If using fresh sheets you will only need to blanch them for 1–2 minutes; dried will need about 5 minutes (check the packet instructions). Using tongs or a spatula, remove the blanched pasta from the pan and place in the bowl of cold water until the sheets are cool enough to handle. Remove to the clean tea towel and leave to dry flat while you prepare the bechamel. Place a second tea towel on top of the sheets if you don't have space to spread them all out in one layer.

BECHAMEL

1 litre (34 fl oz) full-fat milk

75 g (2¾ oz) unsalted butter

75 g (2¾ oz) '00' flour

80 g (2¾ oz) parmesan, finely grated

¼ whole nutmeg, finely grated

sea salt and freshly ground black pepper

grated zest of 1 lemon

Preheat the oven to 180°C (350°F) fan-forced. Lightly oil a 34 x 27 cm (13½ x 10¾ inch) baking dish or roasting tin.

To make the bechamel, pour the milk into a large saucepan and place over a high heat until it is on the edge of boiling, then remove from the heat.

Melt the butter in a second saucepan over a medium heat, then gradually add the flour, a tablespoon at a time, stirring constantly with a wooden spoon. You want the flour and butter to amalgamate and sizzle, creating a paste (roux) that starts to come away from the side of the pan.

Add a ladleful of the hot milk to the roux, along with the parmesan, nutmeg, salt and pepper. Remove the pan from the heat and stir until smooth, then gradually add the remaining milk, stirring constantly. To prevent lumps forming, make sure the mixture is completely smooth before adding more liquid.

Once you have added all the milk, place the pan over a low heat and bring the bechamel to a simmer, stirring constantly until it is thick and creamy. Remove from the heat, stir through the lemon zest and adjust the seasoning if needed. Set aside.

Now you are ready to assemble the lasagne. Line the bottom of the prepared dish or tin with two or three lasagne sheets so the base is completely covered. Spoon half the zucchini sauce over the sheets and smooth out evenly with the back of a spoon. Add about a third of the bechamel and spread it out evenly. Repeat with another layer of pasta, the remaining zucchini mixture and half the remaining bechamel, then finish with a final layer of lasagne sheets, making sure they stick up slightly around the edges. Spread with the last of the bechamel and finish with the grated parmesan.

Place the lasagne in the oven and bake for 30–35 minutes until the top is golden and bubbling. Remove and rest for 15 minutes before serving.

This is even better eaten a day or two after it's prepared as all the flavours have had time to develop and amalgamate. It also freezes very well. Simply assemble the lasagne, top with a piece of baking parchment and put in the freezer. When you are ready to cook it, thaw the lasagne in the fridge overnight then bake as above, adding another 10 minutes to the cooking time.

VARIATION

WITH RICOTTA:– Whisk together 500 g (1 lb 2 oz) of drained ricotta, 2 tablespoons of olive oil, a little grated nutmeg and a generous pinch of salt and pepper in a bowl. Add 100 g (3½ oz) of finely grated parmesan and whisk until combined, then taste for seasoning and adjust if necessary. Use the ricotta mixture in place of the bechamel when assembling the lasagne. Top with 125 g (4½ oz) sliced mozzarella, followed by the parmesan, and bake as instructed.

NOTE

LASAGNE SHEETS:– Nowadays in Italy you can buy really wonderful fresh lasagne sheets from the fridge section in the supermarket. Elsewhere you can usually buy fresh pasta in a similar section but the sheets are never as thin as the ones in Italy so it is imperative to blanch them first, as described in the method. If you skip this step the whole thing will go mushy and spongy, particularly if you are using dried sheets as the pasta will soak up the sauce. You could of course make your own lasagne sheets, but I find that adds a whole other step to this dish that I never have the time or inclination to do.

Involtini di melanzane e pasta

BAKED AUBERGINE WITH PASTA, MOZZARELLA AND TOMATOES

This recipe was taught to me by a woman in Sicily when I was twenty-one. I was a student at the time and couldn't believe the patience it took to complete each step, being much more of an instant gratification sort of cook in those days. But once assembling the involtini (rolls) was underway, it became a pleasantly meditative process. When it came out of the oven it was so delicious that I have never looked back and often make it for gatherings. This dish really benefits from having a very thin pasta, such as angel hair, capellini or vermicelli; linguine works too, but I find it slightly throws off the balance of textures.

PREPARATION:– 30 minutes, plus standing time
COOKING:– 1 hour 20 minutes

SERVES 6

3 large aubergines

sea salt and freshly ground black pepper

80 ml (2½ fl oz) olive oil, plus extra for drizzling

1 garlic clove, peeled and lightly squashed with the edge of a knife

2 good handfuls of basil leaves

2 x 400 g (14 oz) tins peeled plum tomatoes

200 g (7 oz) Capelli d'angelo, capellini, vermicelli or any extremely thin long pasta

80 g (2¾ oz) parmesan, finely grated, plus extra to serve

3 large balls of fior di latte mozzarella, sliced

Trim the ends off the aubergines, then cut lengthways into slices no thicker than 1 cm (½ inch). Sprinkle generously with salt on both sides, place in a colander in the sink and leave for 1 hour.

Meanwhile, heat 2 tablespoons of olive oil, the garlic, a few basil leaves and a pinch of salt in a large saucepan over a medium heat until gently sizzling. Add the tinned tomatoes, then half-fill the empty tins with water and swish it around to pick up any remaining tomato and pour the tomatoey water into the pan. Gently break up the peeled tomatoes with a wooden spoon. Cook for 30 minutes, stirring occasionally, until the liquid has reduced by a third. Remove and discard the garlic clove. Add an extra drizzle of olive oil and a pinch of salt and set aside.

Bring a large saucepan of salted water to the boil. Add the pasta, give it a good stir so it doesn't stick together, and cook for 1 minute less than the packet instructions specify for al dente (it will finish cooking in the oven). Drain the pasta, and toss it with the remaining 50 ml (1¾ fl oz) olive oil, a handful of torn basil leaves, the grated parmesan and a pinch of salt and pepper. Set aside until cool enough to handle.

Pat the aubergine slices with paper towel to remove any excess moisture. Place a chargrill pan over high heat and let it get piping hot. Working in batches, grill the aubergine slices for about 3 minutes each side until nicely browned with noticeable char lines in the flesh. Transfer the grilled slices to a plate and drizzle with a little extra olive oil. Repeat until you've cooked all the aubergine.

Alternatively, spread out the aubergine on a large baking tray lined with baking parchment, brush with olive oil and roast in a preheated 180°C (350°F) fan-forced oven for 25 minutes.

Before you assemble the involtini, preheat the oven to 180°C (350°F) fan-forced.

Get a medium baking dish that will snugly fit all the involtini (about 30 x 20 cm/ 12 x 8 inches). Lay a slice of aubergine on a chopping board and put a tablespoon of the pasta in the centre. Roll up the aubergine to enclose the pasta and place it in the dish, tucking the ends together underneath. Repeat with the remaining aubergine and pasta. Cover the parcels with the tomato sauce, and scatter generously with extra parmesan and, if you would like, a few more torn basil leaves. Finish with a layer of mozzarella slices and a little more parmesan. Bake for 15–20 minutes until the mozzarella begins to bubble and brown on top. Leave to rest for 5–10 minutes, then take the dish to the table and invite people to help themselves.

DAL MARE

FROM THE SEA

DAL MARE

 Italy has over 6400 kilometres (4000 miles) of coastline, so it is hardly surprising that fish has long been a mainstay of its cuisine. Market stands in any coastal town heave with fascinating creatures: netted bags of rock-coloured clams, deep black mussels and piles of gleaming whole silvery fish. For me, the Italian fish market (and cooking fish at all) is a recent discovery, having grown up inland in Tuscany and being scarred as a child by too much tinned tuna and baccalà, a variety of salt cod that is the stalwart of many Italian larders. These experiences made me think that all fish was of the very 'fishy' long-life kind and for years I proclaimed that I hated fish, saying it brought back memories of the school canteen on a Friday when baccalà alla Livornese was inevitably on the menu and the entire school stank of fish.

The fact that growing up 90 minutes from the coast constitutes 'inland' in Italy shows just how local the food culture is. This is partly due to much of Italy's impenetrable topography, which before the advent of motorways meant fresh fish did not travel inland as it was too difficult to transport. In England, living 80 kilometres (50 miles) from the coast generally gives you access to amazing fresh fish every day, whereas when I was growing up in Tuscany we had access only to the dried or preserved variety. There was the occasional visit from a fish van but if you forgot which day it came – as my mother often did – you either opted for cured fish or, as we did, embraced the more inland Tuscan tradition of meat and bean-heavy dishes. Things have changed and there is now a fishmonger in town quite regularly, something that seemed unthinkable in the early 1990s.

It was only in my late teens that I discovered that fresh fish cooked simply is the absolute opposite in flavour and texture to what I knew. There is nothing more delicious on a hot day by the sea than a whole roasted sea bass or bream caught that morning and dressed with a little olive oil and lemon. The fishy flavours I love best are reflected in these recipes 'from the sea'. Some of the most common fish in Tyrrhenian waters are sea bass and sea bream; bass are fished year-round, while bream are more common in summer and autumn. These delicate white fish are interchangeable in these recipes, depending on what your fishmonger has. Other very common fish in the Tyrrhenian are swordfish, cuttlefish, tuna, red and grey mullet (famous for making bottarga), squid and totani – a squid known as 'Sea arrow' in English and particularly popular in the Aeolian Islands.

Anchovies are a stalwart of Tyrrhenian cooking and are particularly prevalent off the coast of Campania. The town of Cetara is well known for its salted anchovies, which are gutted and packed tightly in barrels with layers of salt immediately after being caught. Whenever I go fishing with experienced locals, there is great excitement if the surface of the water shimmers with anchovies as it means there might be a few bluefin tuna nearby (from April to December). I remember one occasion in particular, while on a small boat off the coast of the Cilento National Park in Campania. Francesco, a local fisherman in the town of Pioppi (famous as the birthplace of the 'Mediterranean diet'), started frantically pointing at a spot a few metres away where seagulls were swooping down as it meant that there were anchovies and therefore tuna. Earlier that morning he had, with his seemingly primitive bamboo fishing rod, caught over 200 small anchovies with almost no effort at all – a reminder of the simple pleasure of catching your own supper.

To my mind, simplicity and freshness are everything when it comes to cooking fish. In this chapter I focus on fish found in the Tyrrhenian Sea but have also applied Tyrrhenian methods to a few fish that you would not normally find here, so be guided by whatever your fishmonger has fresh in that day. When buying fish make sure it is as fresh as possible; this means it smells of nothing but the sea, has gleaming scales and bright, clear eyes.

DAL MARE

Spaghetti alla bottarga

BUTTERY SPAGHETTI WITH BOTTARGA

This is my family's favourite way to enjoy bottarga (dried, cured fish roe) – slathered on buttery spaghetti. A more indulgent version is to liberally grate bottarga over a fresh plate of spaghetti alle vongole, which tastes like swimming in the sea.

PREPARATION:– 5 minutes
COOKING:– 10 minutes

SERVES 6

600 g (1 lb 5 oz) spaghetti

150 g (5½ oz) unsalted butter

4 tablespoons olive oil

1 garlic clove, peeled and lightly squashed with the edge of a knife

80 g (2¾ oz) bottarga (preferably from Orbetello), skin removed

Bring a large saucepan of salted water to the boil. Add the spaghetti, give it a good stir so that it doesn't stick together, and cook until al dente (about 9 minutes, but check the packet instructions).

Meanwhile, combine the butter, olive oil and garlic clove in a wide frying pan over a medium–low heat. Grate in about 10 g (¼ oz) of the bottarga and heat gently for about 5 minutes until the mixture starts to sizzle.

When the spaghetti has been cooking for about 5 minutes, add half a ladleful of the cooking water to the butter and olive oil and turn up the heat so they bubble and amalgamate. Remove and discard the garlic clove.

Using tongs, transfer the cooked pasta from the pan to the butter mixture and toss through. Add a little of the cooking water to help coat the strands if necessary.

Portion the pasta into bowls and grate over the remaining bottarga so each serving is topped with a fine orange dust. Serve immediately.

Le linguine di Alek con acciughe, pangrattato e scorza di limone

ALEK'S LINGUINE WITH ANCHOVY, BREADCRUMBS AND LEMON ZEST

Alek is a Polish/Scottish friend who grew up on the Amalfi Coast, where he now lives with his Hungarian girlfriend, Zsofia, and their cohort of rescue dogs. Zsofia is an architect, famed among local builders for being able to operate a JCB on a steep incline overlooking a sheer cliff. They make an intensely stylish couple; I remember one summer we arranged to have lunch together in Marina del Cantone and they arrived on a tiny rubber dinghy with a powerful outboard motor – their preferred mode of transport when at home. The boat was so small and unassuming, compared with the monster yachts moored in the bay, which somehow made their arrival even more glamorous. We had a wonderful afternoon floating off the islands of Li Galli opposite Positano, squashed onto their little boat and leaping into the sea for prolonged swims.

Alek is a terrific cook. He rustled up this simple but memorable dish once when we were visiting my uncle in Catalonia, proving that it works beautifully wherever you make it.

PREPARATION:– 5 minutes
COOKING:– 20 minutes

SERVES 4

40 g (1½ oz) fine breadcrumbs

25 good-quality anchovy fillets preserved in oil

4 garlic cloves, crushed

100 ml (3½ fl oz) olive oil

sea salt

400 g (14 oz) linguine

grated zest of 2 lemons

handful of flat-leaf parsley, roughly chopped

Toast the breadcrumbs in a small frying pan over a medium heat for 3 minutes or until golden brown. Transfer to a bowl and set aside.

Tip the anchovy fillets and their oil into a small bowl and stir in the garlic. Add to a frying pan large enough to toss all the cooked pasta, along with half the olive oil. Reduce the heat to low and gently heat for 3–5 minutes, allowing the anchovy fillets to melt and disintegrate into the warm oil. Add the rest of the oil and continue to infuse, being careful not to let it sizzle too much and burn.

Meanwhile, bring a large saucepan of salted water to the boil. Add the linguine, give it a good stir so that it doesn't stick together, and cook until al dente (about 9 minutes, but check the packet instructions). Halfway through the cooking time, add half a ladleful of the starchy pasta water to the anchovy oil and let it bubble and amalgamate while the pasta cooks.

Using tongs, transfer the pasta to the frying pan and toss through the anchovy oil, then add the lemon zest. Divide the pasta among four bowls, sprinkle with the chopped parsley and finish with the golden breadcrumbs.

SILVANA'S SAFFRON FISH RISOTTO WITH RED MULLET RAGU

This is the signature dish at my friend Anita's hotel on the island of Salina. Originally hailing from Milan, she and her parents decided to buy a run-down hotel in the place where they spent their summers. It has, of course, taken over their lives. Anita's husband gave up his job in finance to become the hotel's baker (his sourdough is legendary) and her mother, Silvana, is now the hotel chef. Dinner at the Principe is a wonderfully convivial affair, conducted on one long table under a pergola overlooking the Tyrrhenian, with the volcano of Stromboli gently bubbling in the distance. Each morning, Silvana writes that evening's menu on a blackboard in the bar and residents can say whether they would like to join. If they do they are treated to a four-course feast, which regularly includes this delicious fish risotto topped with mullet ragu. She has kindly shared her recipe here. You can fillet the fish yourself or ask your fishmonger to do it for you; alternatively, just buy fillets rather than a whole fish.

If you can't find red mullet then sea bass is a delicious and slightly more economical alternative. You can also use vegetable stock rather than fish stock, which I find really lets the saffron and the fish ragu sing.

PREPARATION:– 15 minutes, plus standing time
COOKING:– 50 minutes

20 g (¾ oz) raisins

pinch of saffron

500 g (1 lb 2 oz) red mullet
or sea bass fillets, skin and
bones removed

sea salt

2 tablespoons olive oil

½ small white onion,
finely chopped

30 g (1 oz) tomato paste

30 g (1 oz) flat-leaf parsley
leaves or fennel fronds,
very finely chopped, plus
extra to serve

20 g (¾ oz) pine nuts

RISOTTO

1 litre (34 fl oz) good
fish or vegetable stock

2 pinches of saffron

80 ml (2½ fl oz) olive oil

1 small white onion,
finely chopped

sea salt

450 g (1 lb) arborio rice

150 ml (5 fl oz) white wine

Place the raisins and saffron in a small bowl and pour over enough cold water to just cover them. Leave to soak and plump up for a few minutes.

Meanwhile, cut the fish fillets into 2 cm (¾ inch) chunks. Season with salt and set aside in a bowl for 5 minutes.

Heat the olive oil in a wide frying pan over a medium heat, add the onion and a pinch of salt and cook until translucent. Add the tomato paste, the raisins and their saffrony soaking water, and the parsley or fennel fronds. Stir well, then reduce the heat to low and cook for about 5 minutes.

Increase the heat to medium, add the fish and cook for 3–4 minutes, turning occasionally to make sure it cooks evenly. At the end, stir through the pine nuts. The fish will break up a bit, which will make it a little more ragu-like.

Set aside while you make the risotto.

Combine the stock and saffron in a saucepan over a medium heat until the saffron dissolves. Remove from the heat as it comes to the boil.

In a separate pan, bring 300 ml (10 fl oz) water to the boil, then switch off the heat. Everyone needs a different quantity of liquid for risotto, depending on the kind of rice, the size of your pan and so on. This is just a back up – you may not need it.

Heat the olive oil in a wide, heavy-based frying pan over a medium heat. Once it starts to sizzle, add the onion and a pinch of salt and cook, stirring occasionally, for 3–5 minutes until the onion is translucent. Add the rice and thoroughly mix until it is well coated in the oil. Increase the heat to high and toast the rice, stirring often, to allow the starchy outer coating to soften and disintegrate; this should take 2–3 minutes.

Pour in the wine and stir until it has all been absorbed into the rice and the alcohol has evaporated. Add a ladleful of the hot stock, then stir until the rice has absorbed it all before adding another ladleful. Repeat this process for 18–20 minutes until most of the liquid has been absorbed. (If you run out of stock, add the boiling water.) Try the rice: it should be cooked but still have a little bite without being chalky. Adjust the seasoning if necessary, depending on how salty your stock is. Remove from the heat.

Spoon the risotto onto individual plates and top with a ladleful of the ragu. Sprinkle with a little chopped parsley or fennel fronds and serve immediately.

BAKED COD WITH CHERRY TOMATOES, LEMON AND CAPERS

Cod is usually found in colder waters but is still found on restaurant menus throughout the Tyrrhenian in the form of baccalà (salt cod). I find baccalà a bore as it needs marinating for 24 hours, otherwise it is so salty it's inedible. It's usually served with a tomato sauce 'alla livornese'. This recipe uses fresh cod and tomatoes so is a fresher, lighter version: it's fragrant and colourful without being too intense and brings together many of the foraged flavours of southern Italy, including capers, tomatoes and oregano.

PREPARATION:– 20 minutes, plus resting time
COOKING:– 40 minutes

SERVES 6

500 g (1 lb 2 oz) cherry tomatoes, cut in half lengthways

3 tablespoons brined capers, rinsed

130 g (4½ oz) good-quality black olives, pitted and cut in half

9 garlic cloves, finely sliced

2 lemons, zest grated, then sliced into 1 cm (½ inch) thick discs

1 tablespoon oregano leaves

2 tablespoons olive oil, plus extra for drizzling

sea salt and freshly ground black pepper

800 g (1 lb 12 oz) cod fillets, skinned, pin-boned and cut into 6 even portions

Preheat the oven to 200°C (400°F) fan-forced.

Toss together the tomatoes, capers, olives, garlic, lemon zest and slices, oregano and olive oil in a large roasting tin. Add a generous pinch of salt and a few grinds of pepper and toss again. Bake for about 25 minutes until the tomato skins start to split and the juices are released into the tin.

Remove from the oven and gently place the cod fillets on the tomato mixture. Drizzle a little extra olive oil over each portion and return to the oven. Bake for 12–15 minutes until the fish is white and flaky. If you think it needs longer, bake for another 2–3 minutes and check again.

When the fish is ready, let it rest for about 5 minutes, then take to the table and serve straight from the tin. Part of the beauty of this dish is that you have a ready-made vegetable accompaniment (the tomatoes), but I often add a side of Hasselback 'hedgehog' potatoes (see page 188). If you are eating leftovers the next day, I recommend removing the lemon slices as they will have become very bitter and peely.

THE BAY OF NAPLES

 According to Barone Fabio Colucci, a jovial white-haired Sorrentino with a thick Neapolitan accent, 'I napoletani mangiano come matti' (Neapolitans eat like crazy). He told us this as we wound our way up the hillside above Sorrento in his golf buggy, the seemingly preferred mode of transport for many locals. He was taking us to his ancestral home which sits among olive and lemon groves and enjoys far-reaching views of Capri to the left with the other islands of Ischia and Procida to the right, and Naples and Vesuvius even further round.

As he drove, he casually recounted millennia of Sorrentine history: from the Neolithic, to the Greeks, to the Ottoman invasions, to the Allied occupation during World War II – all in the seventeen-minute journey to his family's palazzo. When I asked what he believes has been the greatest influence on Neapolitan food, Fabio said it is a cuisine born from poverty and greed. Naples has always been poor and hungry, or at least depicted as such, but they also absolutely love their food. It is home to one of my favourite dishes, which I turn to when feeling thrifty and hungry – aglio, olio e pepperoncino (pasta with garlic, chilli and oil), topped with breadcrumbs to mimic the more expensive parmesan.

Neapolitan cuisine is all about making the most of the amazing ingredients they have at their disposal – grown in rich, black volcanic soil on the lower slopes of the still-active Vesuvius – along with patient slow-cooking to maximise their flavours. It seems that Neapolitans are also keen on sex; one of their most famous sauces is the classic puttanesca, a word derived from 'puttana' (prostitute), for reasons so imaginative and varied that it's best to quietly draw your own conclusions. Many Campanian dishes are enriched with cheap and plentiful local anchovies, or even just the liquid that the anchovies have been sitting in, known as colatura di acciughe, illustrating this region's frugality in the kitchen. When cooking meat, families squeeze every last inch of nutrition and flavour out of it. Whole cuts are very slowly cooked in tomato sauce, or in lots of onions as with Naples' famous pasta alla Genovese. The sauce is then used to dress the first course of pasta, and the slow-cooked joint is served as the main course.

Fabio told me of epic Sunday lunches, which are like a Christmas feast on a weekly basis. It happened to be a Sunday afternoon when I was visiting him and he said that at that very moment, families across Campania would be sitting down to an eating marathon: antipasto, a pasta course, a fish dish, a main course and then several desserts, which will have taken all morning to make. Fabio's mother and grandmother used to get up at 4 am to make the meat and tomato ragu for the pasta, which would be reduced and thickened until it was almost black and wonderfully rich.

Desserts are where the Campanians really show off their creativity. There is a rich tradition of baking and pastry in Naples (and Campania generally), largely because Neapolitans have an intensely sweet tooth, but also because they inherited traditions from the settlers and invaders who ran the city at various times. For example, the famous Neapolitan rum baba originates from the Eastern European babka, which came to Naples through the patisserie chefs of Paris (although Fabio argues the Neapolitans improved it enormously).

There is also a tradition of impossibly complicated baking, such as the crunchy, flaky sfogliatella – a cone-shaped treat made from puff pastry coiled over itself to look like a hedgehog, stuffed with a delicious ricotta and semolina filling. Invented by monks on the Amalfi Coast at the Monastero Santa Rosa, this is one of the most iconic sweets of Naples, but it's definitely best left to the experts rather than attempt to make it at home. There is a shortcrust pastry version (see page 216) that I sometimes make as a pie for dinner parties – it's delicious but not nearly as flaky or satisfying.

When entering Campania by land from the north, one crosses the border with Lazio and starts the southerly descent along a 350-kilometre (220 mile) stretch of beautiful Tyrrhenian coastline – at which point it really feels like you are entering l'Italia Meridionale (southern Italy). The region of Caserta is famous for its royal palace, commissioned by King Charles III of Bourbon. The palace was the main royal residence in the 18th century and was later used as the Allied headquarters during the German occupation in World War II (the German surrender was actually signed there in 1945). Its splendour is extraordinary and well worth a visit. Continue down to the fabulous chaos that is the city of Naples, sprawled along the base of perfectly conical Mount Vesuvius. Naples is all busy roads, honking cars, ragged baroque palaces, fascinating museums and incredible market stalls, featuring produce grown in the mineral-rich volcanic soil surrounding Vesuvius.

Abundantly stocked market stalls become a familiar apparition as you explore the Campanian coast, particularly across the bay from the promontory town of Sorrento and the islands of Ischia and Procida. Vesuvius is considered to be one of the most dangerous active volcanoes in the world, due to its proximity to densely populated areas. The amazingly preserved cities of Pompeii and Herculaneum (destroyed in the eruption of 79 CE) serve as sad reminders of the risk for those who live in its shadow. Given that it last erupted in 1943 during the Allied occupation of southern Italy, another eruption is well overdue. Were I to live under a volcano, my preference would be to live under Mount Etna in Sicily, which bubbles and erupts regularly and is therefore less fearsome than Vesuvius, which goes off like a pressure cooker every sixty years or so. On the plus side, there are enormous benefits to living on volcanic soil. Chalky and filled with minerals, it's an incredibly fertile environment for growing San Marzano tomatoes, apricots, artichokes, zucchini, aubergines, brassicas, olives and lemons, not to mention grapes for Greco di Tufo and Avellino wines.

For millenia, Naples has been a key point of trading routes in the Mediterranean. The Greeks settled here in 800 BCE, creating a 'new city' or neo polis, from which the name Napoli derives. The Etruscans followed and later the Romans, who organised the region's cities, giving way eventually to the Byzantines, who are responsible for some of the glorious churches along the Amalfi Coast. The Romans knew Naples as Campania Felix (roughly translated as 'Happy Campania' or 'Fortunate Campania') due to the fertility of its lands. Naples eventually became one of the most important cities in Europe when it came under Spanish rule in 1735 and, following the Napoleonic Wars in 1815, Campania combined with Sicily to become the Kingdom of the Two Sicilies.

Thanks to its long and varied history, Naples became a melting pot of settlers who brought their own culinary traditions. The Unification of Italy in 1861 signalled an end to its era of prosperity, as heavy taxation was introduced from the country's new capital, Rome. Sixty years later Campania suffered terribly during the war, following the Allied landings at Salerno. It became the stage for intense fighting and was heavily bombed by the retreating Germans and advancing Allies; by 1943 much of its produce was destroyed, with even herds of prized water buffalo reared for making mozzarella being slaughtered.

Although it took time for Naples and Campania to recover from the ravages of World War II, recover it did, thanks to its unparalleled beauty and reinvention as one of the most popular holiday spots in the world. Of course, Campania wasn't an entirely undiscovered pocket for passing travellers. Dickens, Goethe, Wagner, Nietzsche and Oscar Wilde all spent time here, while Keats's memorable words, 'vedi Napoli e poi muori' (see Naples then die) have become one of the city's most famous aphorisms.

While Naples today can seem a little dirty and less well maintained than other Italian cities, it retains a romance and a sense of excitement. Very much a working city, the port is one of the most important in Europe, as evidenced by the sprawling dockyards and vast container ships that chug daily across the Bay of Naples. Whenever you get the chance in Italy, travel by water. I did so to Sorrento on the hydrofoil and was rewarded by the most magical journey across the Bay – Vesuvius to the left, the far silhouettes of Capri, Ischia and Procida to the right. Sorrento is a year-round town, although it really comes to life in the summer, when its vast hotels and restaurants can accommodate thousands of tourists drawn by its glorious position, enchanting views and lovely climate.

Along the narrow winding roads leading up from Sorrento into the surrounding rural hills there are many little shrines depicting the Madonna, with small candles in front and often a bunch of flowers or foraged greenery. These shrines are a southern Italian tradition known as 'edicole votive', created specifically to house small candles to shed light on the darkest streets in Naples and later in the surrounding countryside. In the second half of the 18th century, when Naples was ruled by Ferdinand IV of Bourbon, they decided to combat the considerable criminal activity in Naples by artificially lighting the city's main streets with lanterns. Although this did reduce criminality in those areas, it simply drove it to Naples' periphery, making those areas extremely dangerous.

A Dominican monk named Padre Gregorio Maria Rocco proposed a simple solution, which he believed would be effective without costing the Crown an arm and a leg. Finding an unimportant painting of the Madonna in the basement of the Palazzo Reale, he ordered hundreds of colour copies which he installed throughout the city and surrounding areas. He then told locals that those who really wanted to show their love for the Virgin and Christ would always keep her lit up, thus passing on the cost of burning candles every night to the inhabitants of each street. From then on, whenever a loved one would leave the house for a journey or even to complete a simple errand, they would be sent off with the affectionate phrase 'A Madonna t'accompagna' (May the Madonna be with you), which is still one of the most used missives in Campania today. This is just one example of what makes southern Italy – mysticism and traditions that somehow survive, even in our secular, cynical age, sprinkling a touch of magic over the everyday.

Zuppa di cozze alla Cilentana

MUSSEL SOUP WITH TOMATOES, PARSLEY AND GARLIC

This is my recreation of a dish I ate on a strangely warm Saturday in late October, overlooking the sea in San Marco di Castellabate in the Cilento. When the bowl arrived I was first struck by the rich red liquid the mussels sat in, and then by the flavour, which was staggering in its delicious simplicity. It quietly lets the mussels sing. I'm not sure what exactly makes this soup 'Cilentana' as the waiter couldn't tell me, and it seems very similar to a 'Napoletana' version I once had, but I love it anyway. The toasted bread is essential for mopping up the fabulous tomatoey juices from the bowl – choose a crusty loaf that will toast up nicely.

Many find the idea of cooking fresh mussels daunting, but I assure you they are supremely easy to prepare. They just need to be as fresh as possible; in fact, they should be alive when you buy them and eaten the same day. If you have a longish journey home, ask your fishmonger for some ice to keep the mussels cool. Another tip is not to store them in a plastic bag. It's fine to transport them from the shop in one, but as soon as you get home store the mussels in a colander over a large bowl in the fridge until you're ready to start cooking. If you are making this quiet little showstopper for friends, you can make the tomato soup up to three days ahead of time and keep it in the fridge, then reheat and add the mussels at the last minute.

PREPARATION:– 25 minutes
COOKING:– 50 minutes

SERVES 6

75 ml (2½ fl oz) olive oil

3 garlic cloves, peeled and left whole

1 white onion, finely chopped

sea salt

large handful of flat-leaf parsley, leaves picked and finely chopped

800 g (1 lb 12 oz) tin peeled plum tomatoes

3 kg (6 lb 10 oz) fresh mussels

300 ml (10 fl oz) white wine (optional)

crusty white bread, to serve

Choose a very large saucepan with a tight-fitting lid that is at least twice the size of the mussels as they will take up more space once they steam open. Alternatively, use two smaller pans, but still as large as you can manage.

Pour the olive oil into the pan and heat over a medium heat – if you are using one enormous pan add 2 tablespoons water to prevent the garlic from burning. Add the garlic and let it gently cook and infuse for 1–2 minutes, turning the cloves occasionally. Add the onion with a generous pinch of salt and cook for about 5 minutes, stirring frequently, until softened but not coloured. If the onion starts browning, add 50 ml (1¾ fl oz) water to the pan.

Add the parsley, tinned tomatoes and another generous pinch of salt. Half-fill the empty tin with water, swish it around to pick up any remaining tomato and pour the tomatoey water into the pan. Use a wooden spoon to break up the tomatoes as much as possible, then partially cover and simmer over a medium heat for 30 minutes, stirring occasionally, adding 150 ml (5 fl oz) water halfway through.

Meanwhile, rinse each mussel individually under cold running water, discarding any that are already open, have a majorly cracked shell or do not close when you tap them. Horrid to say, but mussels should be alive at the point of cooking. Scrub the shells to remove any barnacle-type bits and remove the 'beard' by giving it a sharp tug towards the thinner end of the mussel.

Preheat the oven to 150°C (300°F) fan-forced.

Add the mussels to the bubbling tomato liquid, along with the wine if using, and stir thoroughly to make sure that they are well coated. Cover and steam over a medium heat for 10–12 minutes (very large mussels will need the full 12 minutes), stirring once or twice to make sure they are well coated in the liquid.

Meanwhile, slice the bread and place on a baking tray. Bake for 5–10 minutes, turning over halfway through, until completely dried out and golden. Remove from the oven.

As soon as the mussels have opened, ladle them into bowls with a generous amount of the tomato broth. Serve with the toast. Don't forget to have extra bowls on hand for discarded mussel shells.

Tonno alla griglia con piselli freschi

GRILLED TUNA STEAKS WITH FRESH PEAS AND SALSA VERDE

This is based on a classic recipe from Elba called Palamita di Elba. Palamita is Italian for bonito fish – a dark, oily fish related to mackerel and tuna which is very common in the Tyrrhenian, passing through its waters from spring to autumn on the hunt for sardines and anchovies. The spring arrival of bonito in the Tyrrhenian coincides with the first spring peas, which is celebrated by the inhabitants of Elba in this dish. Bonito is often incorrectly said to be the 'poor man's tuna', but it has a compact strong-tasting meat which true fish lovers adore. I prefer a meaty tuna steak, which is why I reinterpreted the recipe. Swordfish and mackerel also work well, as would, of course, bonito.

PREPARATION:– 15 minutes
COOKING:– 25 minutes

SERVES 6

4 tablespoons olive oil, plus extra to serve

1 white onion, finely chopped

sea salt and freshly ground black pepper

1 garlic clove, crushed

500 g (1 lb 2 oz) shelled peas (about 1 kg/2 lb 3 oz in pods) or frozen peas

handful of flat-leaf parsley and mint leaves, roughly chopped

150 ml (5 fl oz) white wine

6 tuna steaks, ideally 1 cm (½ inch) thick

90 g (3 oz) Salsa verde (see page 70)

Heat 3 tablespoons of olive oil in a wide frying pan over a medium heat. Once it starts to sizzle, add the onion and a good pinch of salt and cook, stirring occasionally, for 3–5 minutes until the onion is translucent. Stir in the garlic and cook for another 2 minutes or so. Add the peas, half the herbs, another pinch of salt and a few grinds of pepper. Stir and leave to sizzle for a minute, then pour in the wine and enough water to just cover the peas. Reduce the heat and simmer gently for 15 minutes or until the peas are tender but still retain their lovely green colour. (This will take half the time if you're using frozen peas.) Add the rest of the herbs, then taste and adjust the seasoning if necessary. Remove from the heat and set aside.

Place a chargrill pan or frying pan over a high heat on your hottest hob. Meanwhile, dab your tuna steaks on both sides with paper towel or a clean tea towel to remove any excess moisture. Brush with a little oil and lightly season on both sides with salt and pepper.

While the pan is heating up, transfer the peas to a serving dish and drizzle over a little more olive oil.

Place the steaks in the piping-hot pan and sear for 45–60 seconds on each side, depending on their thickness. You just want them to brown on the outside while remaining pink in the middle. Arrange the tuna on the bed of peas and spoon a generous tablespoon of salsa verde over each steak. Serve straight away.

DELICIOUS WITH:– Garlicky grilled tomatoes; Crispy new potatoes with capers or Hasselback 'hedgehog' potatoes (see pages 176, 187 and 188).

WHOLE SEA BREAM COOKED 'IN PARCELS' WITH LEMON, THYME AND OLIVES

Pesce in cartoccio (fish baked in baking parchment parcels) is cooked all along the Tyrrhenian coast in a variety of ways. It's so satisfying as you can prepare a whole meal within the parcels by placing your side dish at the base and popping the fillets on top, and because the fish is steamed inside the baking parchment the result is deliciously succulent. It also minimises washing up, which I am always a fan of. This recipe features a combination of southern Italian ingredients I particularly love (olives, thyme, chilli and lemon), but once you have mastered the basic method, feel free to experiment with your own flavours and accompaniments.

PREPARATION:– 30 minutes, plus standing time
COOKING:– 50 minutes

SERVES 4

300 g (10½ oz) good-quality black olives (I like Italian Leccino or Greek Kalamata), pitted and finely chopped

2 garlic cloves, finely chopped

a few thyme sprigs, leaves picked

½ long red chilli, deseeded and finely chopped (or a pinch of chilli flakes)

2 lemons, zest grated, then sliced into thin discs

juice of ½ lemon

100 ml (3½ fl oz) olive oil

sea salt and freshly ground black pepper

1.2 kg (2 lb 10 oz) new potatoes, peeled and sliced into quarters if small, or 4 cm (1½ inch) chunks if large

2 whole sea bream (about 550 g/1 lb 3 oz each), gutted and scaled

150 ml (5 fl oz) dry white wine

Preheat the oven to 180°C (350°F) fan-forced.

In a bowl, mix together the olives, garlic, thyme, chilli, lemon zest and juice, half the olive oil and a pinch of salt. Set aside while you prepare the potatoes and fish parcels.

Place the potatoes in a roasting tin large enough to fit the pieces in a single layer, and toss with the remaining olive oil and a generous sprinkling of salt. Roast in the oven for 10 minutes while you prepare the fish parcels.

Rinse the sea bream under cold running water inside and out, then pat dry with a clean tea towel. If the fish still has its fins, remove these with scissors or a sharp knife at the root.

Cut two pieces of baking parchment and foil large enough to wrap and seal around the fish. Place the foil pieces on a bench and top with the baking parchment, then put one fish in the middle of each and season inside and out with salt and pepper.

Lift the foil and parchment up around the fish slightly and spoon some of the olive mixture into each cavity, along with two slices of lemon, then spoon the rest of the olive mix on top. Finish off with two more lemon slices. Pour equal amounts of wine over each fish, then seal the baking parchment tightly by pinching the ends together and twisting over. Repeat with the foil to make sure no steam escapes.

Take the potatoes out of the oven, place the parcels on top and bake for 40 minutes. (If you don't have a roasting tin large enough, divide the potatoes between two and perch a parcel on top of each.) Remove from the oven, take off the parcels and transfer to a chopping board to rest for 10 minutes. Toss the potatoes and return to the oven to crisp up while the fish rests. When they are ready, transfer to a serving dish. Carefully unwrap the fish parcels, taking care to reserve the cooking liquid. Fillet the fish and serve with the potatoes, plenty of the olive mixture and the cooking liquid.

> **DELICIOUS WITH:–** Garlicky grilled tomatoes and Grilled zucchini with garlic and chilli (see pages 176 and 186).

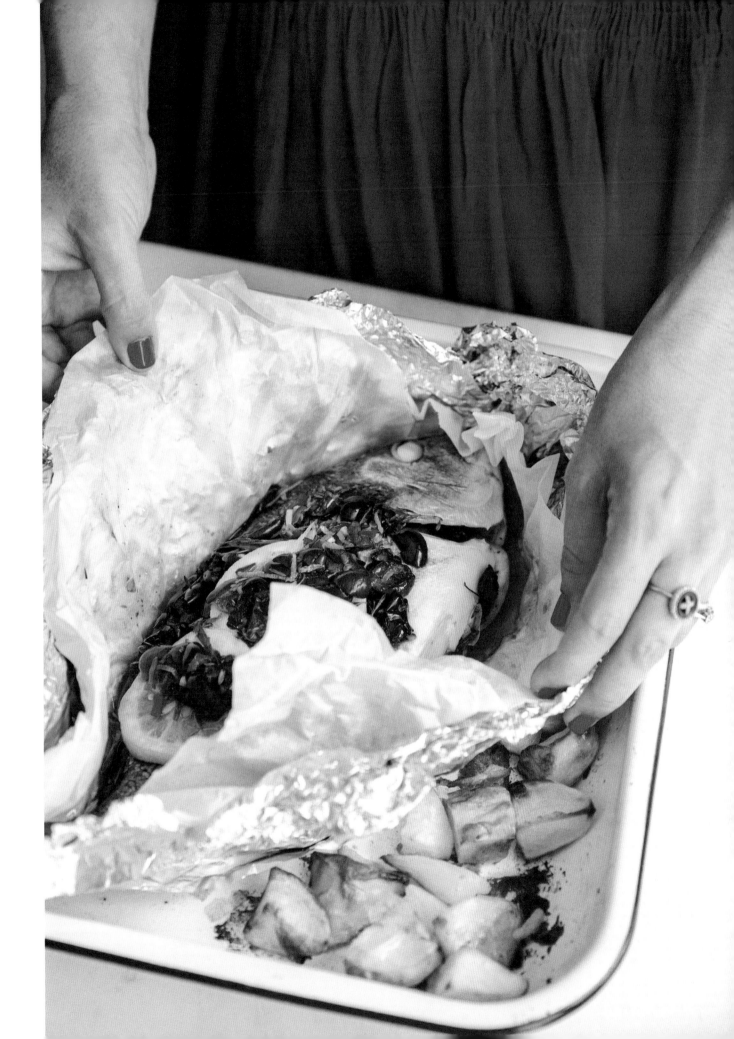

TWO NUTTY FISH FILLETS

This is my go-to method if I'm cooking white fish for friends or just want to make something that is easy but looks impressive. I came across the first recipe at Le Scalette beach shack in Sabaudia, the Fascist-era resort in Lazio, where they were serving a fillet of sea bream hidden under a mound of almond flakes. The second recipe is based on a dish I first saw in Sicily, where a fishmonger was selling pre-prepared sea bass fillets topped with ground pistachios and sun-dried tomatoes. Initially I was simply struck by the vibrancy of the green, white and red colours, then realised how much I would love the combination of flavours. Both dishes are fabulous: salty and nutty, with a divine textural contrast between the tender white fish and the crunchy nuts, which become toasted as the fish bakes. You can use either sea bream or sea bass in both recipes.

SABAUDIA, LAZIO

Orata in crosta di mandorle

BAKED SEA BREAM WITH ALMOND FLAKES

PREPARATION:– 15 minutes
COOKING:– 10 minutes

SERVES 4

100 g (3½ oz) flaked almonds

1 tablespoon fine breadcrumbs

1 lemon

sea salt and freshly ground black pepper

2 tablespoons olive oil, plus extra for brushing

4 large sea bream fillets, pin-boned

Preheat the oven to 180°C (350°F) fan-forced.

In a bowl, toss together the flaked almonds, breadcrumbs, a light grating of lemon zest, a generous pinch of salt and 1 tablespoon olive oil.

Line a roasting tin with baking parchment and brush with a little olive oil so the fish won't stick. Add the fish fillets, skin side down, and season with salt and pepper. Drizzle over the remaining olive oil and a light squeeze of lemon juice (save the rest to serve). Evenly spoon the almond mixture over the fillets, making sure they are completely covered.

Bake for 10 minutes or until the fish is white and flaky. Remove from the oven, finish with a final squeeze of lemon juice and serve immediately.

DAL MARE

Spigola con pistacchi, pinoli e pomodori secchi

SEA BASS WITH PISTACHIOS, PINE NUTS AND SUN-DRIED TOMATOES

PREPARATION:– 15 minutes
COOKING:– 10 minutes

SERVES 4

50 g (1¾ oz) unsalted pistachios

2 tablespoons olive oil, plus extra for brushing

4 large sea bass fillets, pin-boned

sea salt and freshly ground black pepper

6 large sun-dried tomatoes in oil, drained and finely chopped

2 tablespoons pine nuts

Preheat the oven to 180°C (350°F) fan-forced.

Blitz the pistachios in a food processor to a chunky, coarse consistency. Set aside in a small bowl.

Line a roasting tin with baking parchment and brush with a little olive oil so the fish won't stick. Add the fish fillets, skin side down, and season with salt and pepper. Evenly sprinkle a heaped teaspoon of the ground pistachio over each fillet, and top with a teaspoon of sun-dried tomato, a few pine nuts, a little salt and pepper and a drizzle of olive oil.

Bake for 10–11 minutes or until the fish is white and flaky. Remove from the oven and serve immediately.

DELICIOUS WITH:– Garlicky grilled tomatoes; Crispy new potatoes with capers; Neapolitan vinegary fried zucchini (see pages 176, 187 and 184) or your choice of grilled vegetables.

NOTE:– I often serve both of these fish dishes with the simplest potatoes pictured here. One large potato per person cut into superfine discs, tossed with 1 tablespoon of olive oil and a generous pinch of sea salt and roasted in a hot oven for about 20 minutes.

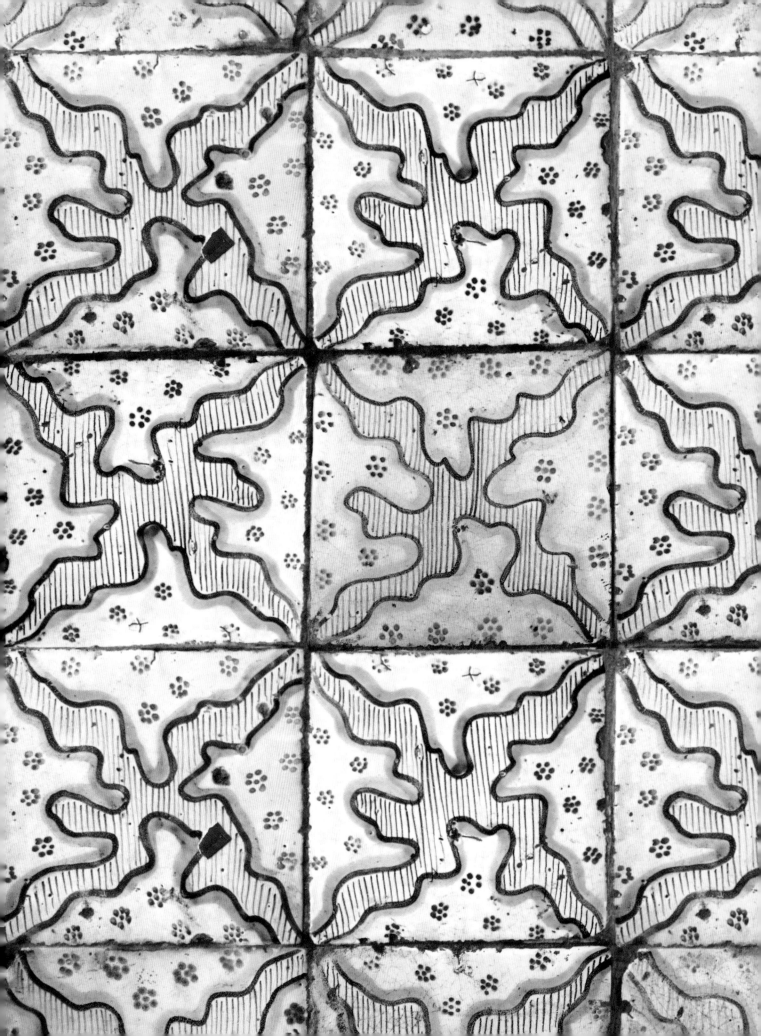

DALLA TERRA

FROM THE LAND

DALLA TERRA

 Much of this book is about summer, a time for fish and salads and vegetables. But there are some dishes from the Tyrrhenian region that call for meat, especially in the Maremma, Tuscany's long and wild coast. Here, meat sits at the heart of traditional cooking. Foraging and hunting was and is a big part of life on Tuscany's southern coast, and one of my favourite dishes is penne alla buttera (see page 156), a sausage and olive sauce allegedly made by local cowboys who herded buffalo on horseback.

Buffalo are an important part of the west coast's economy and cuisine, though the days when its meat was a delicacy prized by the nobility are long gone. Today they are reared in Tuscany, Lazio and Campania for their milk, used to make delicious mozzarella and burrata. Indeed, these fresh, light cheeses are one of western Italy's great contributions to world gastronomy. The French excel at making strong cheeses, but Italians lean towards light, subtle flavours – mozzarella, pecorino and that delicious, zero-waste by-product, ricotta – all ingenious ways of using sheep and buffalo milk.

Further south on Italy's western coast, where the terrain is rougher, meat was not historically consumed very often because the cliffs were too sheer to accommodate livestock and it was difficult to travel inland to buy it. It was the same on remote islands such as Ponza, Ischia, Capri and the Aeolians. There simply wasn't the space to keep cattle, though they have always bred chickens and rabbits, hence the island of Ischia's famous dish coniglio all'Ischitana and Ponza's coniglio alla Ponzese. Any larger cuts of meat that do make their way to these remote places will be dressed with whatever is available locally. On the Sicilian islands the butcher will have counters of pork chops and meatballs stuffed with capers and coated in chopped nuts, and chicken is often cooked with lemon in Sicily and Campania, Italy's lemon-growing capitals.

On the larger islands of Sicily and Sardinia, there is plenty of space for grazing so livestock has always been part of the inland cuisine. The Sicilians are very keen on horse meat and offal, which are not my favourite, though they are a very sustainable way of consuming meat. In Catania on Sicily's eastern coast facing the Ionian Sea, there are endless market stalls selling braised horsemeat sandwiches, which my friend Emily will always gamely try while I shudder pathetically behind her.

Though I am not a vegetarian, I have definitely followed the trend of consuming less meat. When I do have meat I want to have its best possible form, complemented by exquisite flavours. I therefore shop with the intent of finding the best I can afford and talk to my butcher about the provenance of what I'm buying. Some of Italy's best meat dishes are from this region and capitalise on the local ingredients of capers, anchovies, tomatoes, pistachios, lemons and zucchini, so the recipes that follow celebrate meat, and a little ricotta, using the Tyrrhenian palate.

Gnocchi di ricotta alla Sorrentina

RICOTTA GNOCCHI IN TOMATO AND MOZZARELLA SAUCE

This dish is emblematic of the jaunty seaside town of Sorrento overlooking the Bay of Naples: pillowy potato gnocchi poached in tomato sauce and tossed in mozzarella with a little parmesan. It's greedy and delicious, but my version uses ricotta gnocchi infused with a little lemon zest and basil to make it lighter and more fragrant. If you're having people over, you can make the gnocchi and tomato sauce ahead of time, then poach the gnocchi and warm the tomato sauce just before serving. Shaping the gnocchi can be a fun meditative task to do on your own, or put your friends to work, creating a jolly, convivial meal that everyone has helped prepare. If you don't have time to make the gnocchi, 500 g (1 lb 2 oz) shop-bought potato gnocchi will work well too.

PREPARATION:– 30 minutes, plus resting time
COOKING:– 40 minutes

SERVES 6

3 tablespoons olive oil, plus extra for drizzling

1 garlic clove, peeled and lightly squashed with the edge of a knife

sea salt

handful of basil leaves, roughly torn

2 x 400 g (14 oz) tins peeled plum tomatoes

2 large balls of fior di latte mozzarella, drained and torn into small pieces

grated zest of 1 lemon

GNOCCHI

750 g (1 lb 11 oz) ricotta, drained

100 g (3½ oz) parmesan, finely grated, plus extra to serve

grated zest of 2 lemons

½ whole nutmeg, finely grated

30 g (1 oz) basil leaves, roughly torn

sea salt and freshly ground black pepper

4 large organic egg yolks

180 g (6½ oz) '00' flour, plus extra for shaping

Start with the tomato sauce. Heat the olive oil in a saucepan over medium heat, add the garlic clove, a pinch of salt and a few basil leaves and heat until gently sizzling. Add the tinned tomatoes, then half-fill the empty tins with water, swish it around to pick up any remaining tomato and pour the tomatoey water into the pan. Break up the peeled tomatoes with a wooden spoon. Cook for 30 minutes, stirring occasionally, until the liquid has reduced by a third. Remove and discard the garlic clove. Add a drizzle of oil and another pinch of salt, then set side.

To make the gnocchi, place the drained ricotta in a large bowl and, using handheld electric beaters, whisk for 1 minute until smooth. Add the parmesan, lemon zest, nutmeg, basil, a generous pinch of salt and a few grinds of pepper. Check the seasoning: you want the dough to be heavily, almost over-seasoned with salt and pepper before the egg yolks go in. When you're happy, whisk in the yolks one by one. Taste for seasoning again and adjust if necessary. The mixture will be quite liquid because of the egg. Gradually stir in the flour, a tablespoon at a time. The dough should be nice and smooth.

Generously dust a clean surface with flour. Dust a large plate or baking tray with flour (this needs to fit in your fridge, so use several smaller plates if necessary) to keep next to you as you work, ready for your shaped gnocchi. Flour your hands too so that the mixture doesn't stick to them.

Scoop out 1 tablespoon of the mixture (about 20 g/¾ oz) and drop onto the floured surface. Roll it in the flour, then pick it up and gently roll it between your palms to make a ball about 2 cm (¾ inch) in diameter. Repeat with the remaining ricotta mixture to make about 45 balls slightly smaller than a golf ball. Cover the gnocchi and place in the fridge to rest for at least 30 minutes, or up to 24 hours if you are serving the next day.

Bring a very large saucepan of salted water to the boil over a high heat to cook your gnocchi (both homemade and shop bought need to be pre-poached).

Meanwhile, heat the tomato sauce over a medium heat. Add the mozzarella pieces and stir through the sauce, then remove from the heat.

Gently drop the gnocchi into the boiling water one by one, making sure you don't overcrowd the pan. They will initially sink to the bottom, but will happily bob to the surface when they are done – this will only take about 2–3 minutes. If they don't appear on the surface, gently nudge them with a wooden spoon to make sure they haven't stuck to the bottom.

When the first batch has floated to the top, use a slotted spoon to fish them out and transfer to the tomato sauce. Repeat with the remaining gnocchi. Gently toss the cooked gnocchi through the sauce – if your pan isn't big enough, transfer everything to a serving dish. Sprinkle generously with extra parmesan, a little grated lemon zest and a good grinding of pepper. Serve immediately.

Penne alla buttera

PENNE WITH COWBOY RAGU

Butteri are cowboys from the southern coastal region of Maremma in Tuscany. Apparently dating back to when the area was run by the Etruscans, butteri were responsible for wrangling the buffalo the region is famous for on horseback. They were central to the economy of Maremma, making the most of the region's varied landscape – marsh, woodland, hills and coast – throughout the year. With the demise of large estates in the 20th century the role became more folkloristic than a way to make a living.

Pasta alla buttera is a quick and practical dish that could be made on the move over a campfire. As with most peasant dishes it was traditionally made with whatever the butteri had to hand (meaning there are a hundred different versions), but generally it featured sausages made of wild boar, which run rampant through the Tuscan countryside. Here I use good-quality pork sausages, and I've allowed a little more cooking time to develop maximum flavour. Do be picky about your sausages as the best you can buy will give a superior texture.

PREPARATION:– 15 minutes
COOKING:– 40 minutes

SERVES 6

6 wild boar or organic pork sausages

3 tablespoons olive oil

½ white onion, finely chopped

sea salt

2 garlic cloves, crushed

1 long red chilli, cut in half lengthways, deseeded and finely sliced crossways into ribbons

130 g (4½ oz) good-quality black olives, pitted and sliced in half lengthways

400 ml (13½ fl oz) tomato passata

500 g (1 lb 2 oz) penne

chilli flakes, to taste

80 g (2¾ oz) pecorino toscano or romano, finely grated, plus extra to serve

Remove the sausage meat from its casings, put in a bowl and break into small bite-sized pieces.

Heat 1 tablespoon of olive oil in a wide frying pan or medium saucepan over a medium heat. Brown the sausage meat for 5 minutes, stirring occasionally to ensure it cooks evenly, then transfer to a bowl.

Heat the remaining olive oil in the pan, add the onion and a pinch of salt and cook over a medium heat for 2 minutes. Add the garlic, sliced chilli and half the olives and cook for another 5 minutes or until the onion is translucent. Stir in the sausage meat.

Pour the passata over the sausage mixture, then half-fill the empty bottle with water and swish it around to pick up any remaining tomato and pour the tomatoey water into the pan. Add the rest of the olives and leave to bubble away over a medium heat for 25 minutes, stirring occasionally.

Meanwhile, bring a large saucepan of salted water to the boil. Add the penne, give it a good stir so that it doesn't stick together, and cook until al dente (about 10 minutes, but check the packet instructions). Halfway through the cooking time, scoop out a ladleful of the starchy pasta water and add it to the sauce. Increase the heat and stir so that the water amalgamates with the sauce. Taste and adjust the seasoning if necessary and add chilli flakes, to taste.

Drain the pasta and add to the sauce, along with the grated pecorino and a splash of pasta water if it still needs help coming together. Serve immediately, topped with more pecorino.

Beachwood Branch

Checked out to 12718259
07/12/2024 12:04

Checked Out Today

Italian coastal
Barcode: 4006702501
Date due: 08/02/2024

Farewell, Amethystine
Barcode: 4006735453
Date due: 08/02/2024

Front sight
Barcode: 4006691940
Date due: 08/02/2024

Branch phone: 216-831-6868

Carpaccio di manzo con zucchine, rucola e pecorino

BEEF CARPACCIO WITH ZUCCHINI, ROCKET AND PECORINO

Carpaccio is an indulgent yet light dish to eat in the warmer summer months. When well executed the beef should be gossamer thin and wonderfully tender. It's also the perfect vehicle for all sorts of toppings, like raw porcini in autumn or an artichoke salad in spring. In summer I love it topped with zesty rocket, fresh discs of raw zucchini and shavings of a strong pecorino or parmesan, all doused in lemon juice and the finest olive oil I can find. This is a typical Tuscan summer dish and I have enjoyed it many times at the beach in the Maremma. This recipe is designed as a main meal, but if you want to serve it as a starter as part of an antipasto platter, just halve the quantities. If you can, ask your butcher to slice the beef for you on their meat slicer; otherwise, follow the instructions below.

PREPARATION:– 15 minutes

SERVES 6

500 g (1 lb 2 oz) beef fillet

sea salt and freshly ground black pepper

50 ml (1¾ fl oz) very good olive oil

juice of ½ lemon

150 g (5½ oz) rocket leaves

2 green or summery yellow zucchini (about 100 g/ 3½ oz each), sliced into thin discs

freshly shaved pecorino, to serve

Using a very sharp knife, cut the beef into slices no thicker than 1 cm (½ inch). Tear off a sheet of baking parchment, place a slice of beef on it and cover with another piece of parchment. Use a rolling pin to roll out the beef to a 2 mm (1⁄16 inch) thickness. Set aside and repeat with the remaining beef.

Arrange the beef slices, overlapping slightly, on a large serving plate. Season lightly with salt and pepper, then drizzle with a little olive oil and a few drops of lemon juice. Scatter over the rocket and top with the zucchini discs. Pour over the remaining lemon juice and olive oil and season with pepper. Finish with freshly shaved shards of pecorino. Serve immediately.

DELICIOUS WITH:– Garlicky grilled tomatoes and Maurizia's potato, olive and caper salad (see pages 176 and 84).

THE AMALFI COAST

The glamour of the Amalfi Coast is world famous, but it is a fleck of gold on the broader canvas of Campania, a vast and varied region that encompasses Naples, Capri, Sorrento and the lesser-known Cilento. Venture beyond the veil of swanky hotels and expensive boat rides and you'll find a dense tapestry of history, culture and contrasting landscapes, with an equally rich culinary tradition. I first discovered its wonders in 2015, when I made a pilgrimage to the town of Amalfi and was immediately mesmerised. Despite being frightening and slightly car-sick inducing, the treacherous winding road along the coast is a wonderful way to see the dramatic landscape, which drops away beneath you into the Tyrrhenian. Seemingly gravity-defying gardens and lemon groves perch along the cliffs on amazingly constructed terraces leading down to pretty fishing villages and secluded swimming spots.

The first thing that struck me about the town of Amalfi was a feeling of life being truly lived. There is a tremendous energy to this jaunty port town, with an exciting hustle and bustle of people and scooters. Our bus deposited us on a big roundabout between the cobbled shopping streets and the beach. Mosaics made from tiles in the nearby town of Vietri sul Mare adorn many of the buildings, directing visitors to various favourite restaurants; cliffs rise up dramatically on both sides of the town and behind it. Amalfi's main square is dominated by the mosaiced 10th-century cathedral of St Andrea, with steep majestic stairs that lead from the piazza to its entrance. The effect is dramatic, particularly when you crane your neck to take in the sheer cliffs that loom up behind the bell tower and domed ceiling. Immediately to the right of the church sits the ever-glamorous Pasticceria Pansa with its mirrored walls, old wooden pharmacy counters, white-gloved waiters and delicious treats such as Delizia al limone and Torta di ricotta e pere (two cakes so delicious that I have replicated them in this book on page 227 and page 212).

Above all, I love the market stalls in Amalfi, especially the dried home-grown chillies that hang from shop doorways with a sign saying 'Viagra naturale – €5 al mazzo' (natural Viagra – 5 euros a bunch). The combination of ancient architecture, colour, spice, citrus and chaos give one the feeling of truly being in the south of Italy. This is particularly true further east in the town of Vietri sul Mare, just at the end of the Amalfi Coast where it gives way to Salerno. This is the ceramic capital of Campania, where you find all the glorious plates and bowls for which this region is renowned. Narrow streets are vividly brought to life by lovely locally painted tiles that mosaic each store front, lending these otherwise dark spaces a vivid riot of colour. The main street gives way to a network of steep narrow alleys hugger-mugger with greengrocers and fishmongers, all with fabulous outdoor tiles depicting groaning buckets of fresh produce. Its proximity to the motorway means that Vietri is a genuine working town rather than exclusively a tourist destination, with people living there all year round. This is not true in other parts of the Amalfi Coast, which shut up shop at the end of the season in mid-November.

Even if you are not eating in one of the coast's many smart restaurants, the dramatic landscape makes even the simplest meal memorable. One such evening that has stayed with me was in Praiano, a less fashionable town halfway between Amalfi and Positano. The town's main landmark, the honey-coloured church of San Gennaro, dominates the roofline with its mosaiced blue, white and orange cupola and onion-shaped bell tower. The church doors are fronted by a large mosaiced piazza, jutting out directly into the sea with nothing beneath it, or so it seemed to us, sitting in the pizzeria just above the piazza.

Pizza in Campania is a serious business. Neapolitan pizza is characterised by a light and airy inner crust (achieved by leaving the dough to rise for twenty-four hours) and a crunchy outside crust, charred from the heat of the pizza oven. A Roman pizza on the other hand tends to be a thinner, crunchier, less doughy affair. Our pizza was, as I have always been told Neapolitan pizza should be, 'appena baciata dal pomodoro' (just kissed by tomato) and topped with plenty of melted mozzarella. As I munched away I was bowled over by the beauty around me: the sun was setting over the bay, the bells of San Gennaro were ringing, and children of Praiano were playing a game of football in the church square. Everything came together over that €8 pizza and birra alla spina (draft beer) to make it a wonderfully memorable moment.

While I appreciated the spectacular natural beauty around me, it was of course the food of the Amalfi Coast that stole my heart on that first visit. This was sparked by a trip to the famous restaurant Da Adolfo, which is only accessible by boat (they provide a shuttle on a small fishing boat from Positano's main port). Once you arrive at this glorious beach shack the best course of action is to rent a sun bed from the restaurant and commit to a day of sunbathing, swimming and feasting. They will happily keep you fuelled with jugs of white wine full of ice and chunks of white peach – the perfect summer aperitivo to get you ready for a lunch of local mozzarella grilled in lemon leaves, delicious fish pastas and chargrilled sea bass. After finishing with a slice of torta caprese al limone (a lemon incarnation of Capri's famous chocolate almond cake), an afternoon of snoozing is the only option for the rest of the day.

The food of the Amalfi Coast differs from that of Naples in that it is fresh, simple and based predominantly on fish. Villages lining the coast sit atop precipitous cliffs that lead down to the water. Reachable by a network of treacherous stairs (which certainly help work off an over-indulgent lunch), this dramatic terrain traditionally meant that the water and terraced orchards were the main sources of food in the bygone leaner days before it became the ultra-successful tourist destination it is today. The unpretentious style of cooking is designed to show off the quality of the ingredients and freshness of the fish, which is usually grilled, roasted or tossed with pasta.

This approach to food is perfectly demonstrated at Lo Scoglio in Marina del Cantone at the far western peak of the Amalfi Coast, almost at the point where the Sorrento and Amalfi coastlines meet. This legendary family-run restaurant sits at the heart of a perfectly curved bay and prides itself on using produce grown on the hillside by Peppino, the father of the family. Each morning he picks whatever is ready to eat and gives it to his son Tommaso in the kitchen to be transformed into a myriad of delicious dishes. Front of house is run by the glamorous Antonia and Margherita, Peppino's two very capable and business-savvy daughters. Their insalata caprese is second to none, and Peppino tells me it is because of the way he grows his tomatoes – organic, with plenty of space and no pesticides. It costs him five times what supermarkets charge for a single tomato, which explains why this is the best – and most expensive – caprese I have ever tasted.

The secluded little town in which the restaurant sits is best reached by boat, as the road from Nerano is long, winding and at times treacherous. To give you a sense of the terrain, Marina del Cantone is around twenty minutes from Positano by boat, but about an hour by road. This is one of my favourite places to stay on the Amalfi Coast as it's more down to earth than Positano and some of the other villages that dot the coastline. Various pizzerias, bars and eateries line the waterfront, and it's possible to rent sun loungers very inexpensively, or even hire a dingy to explore the neighbouring bays.

Continue west by boat from Lo Scoglio and you will find the promontory of Punta Campanella – the point that divides the Amalfi and Sorrento coasts. This area is rich with mythology. It is said to be where Odysseus escaped the bewitched song of the sirens in the twelfth book of Homer's *Odyssey*. You can still see the ruins of the Temple of Athena, said to be built by Odysseus as a thank you to the gods for his narrow escape. According to our friend Fabio, a Sorrentine baron who owns the wonderful Chez Barone cooking school, this myth is so engrained locally that the root of Sorrento's name is in fact the Latin Sirrentum (land of the sirens). For those who don't know it, three beautiful sirens (half women, half fish, though they are sometimes depicted as half birds) were said to live on the promontory. They sang to passing sailors until they were overcome by the desire to follow the enchanted music, ploughing through the Tyrrhenian Sea to reach Punta Campanella where their ships would hit the point's treacherous rocks and sink, drowning all on board.

Odysseus was forewarned of the danger by the witch Circe, who told him to make sure that all his men plugged their ears with wax to block out the enchanted song of the sirens. However, Odysseus was desperately curious and determined to hear the song and survive. Unable to dissuade him, Circe instructed him to tie himself to the mast of the ship and order his men not to release him until they had passed the promontory, even if he begged. And beg he did as they passed the sirens, but as his men couldn't hear him, they escaped unscathed. In a rage, the sirens flung themselves into the sea and drowned, turning into three large rocks which sit together just off the Amalfi Coast, known as Li Galli, or sometimes as Le Sirenuse.

Standing some four miles off the coast from Positano, these three islands provide one of the most heavenly swimming spots in the area, despite their inauspicious start as angry sirens. There is a wonderful, secluded bay in between the islands where people moor their boats to swim, though clambering onto the rocks is strictly prohibited. The largest of the three islands was bought by the Russian ballet choreographer Léonide Massine in 1919. He built a fabulous private villa and turned the ancient watch tower into a dance studio with an open-air theatre. Following his death in the 1980s, the island was bought by another Russian dancer, Rudolf Nureyev, who hosted everyone from Jackie Kennedy to Franco Zeffirelli and Sophia Loren.

I first swam off the islets of Li Galli during our honeymoon and couldn't believe the clarity of the crystal blue waters. We were taken out by a charming boatman called Angelo, who knew everything about local history. He told us that the town of Amalfi had been a hugely successful trading port and an independent maritime republic in the 11th and 12th centuries, rivalling Venice in its control of the luxury goods trades of spices, silks, carpets and perfumes. It fell into decline when it was annexed by the Normans and was later weakened by severe flooding in the 14th century, coupled with a few bouts of plague, which destroyed the coast's prosperity until it was revived by tourism and La Dolce Vita in the 20th century. This history lesson was recounted to us as we bobbed in the bay of Marina del Cantone, Angelo's hometown, which was made all the more magical by the appearance of another boat selling ice-creams and iced coffee, manned by Angelo's father. As we chatted across the two boats over a coffee, I remember feeling incredibly happy as the sun baked and dried the salt on our skin.

Scaloppine alla pizzaiola

VEAL ESCALOPES IN TOMATO SAUCE WITH MOZZARELLA AND ANCHOVY

Fragrant, garlicky and topped with a layer of melted cheese, scaloppine alla pizzaiola is my husband's favourite dish and one we often make at home. Originating from Naples, it takes its name from that other Neapolitan invention – pizza – and was a way for poorer communities to use up old cuts of meat by masking it in a rich tomato sauce. For me, part of the appeal is the speed and ease with which it can be prepared, making it one of those satisfying recipes where minimal effort leads to maximum flavour and enjoyment. If you can't find veal, or prefer not to cook with it, the dish also works well with chicken (see variation, right).

PREPARATION:– 10 minutes, plus standing time
COOKING:– 25 minutes

SERVES 4

4 veal escalopes

1 large ball of fior di latte mozzarella

sea salt and freshly ground black pepper

75 g (2¾ oz) '00' flour

30 g (1 oz) unsalted butter, plus extra if needed

2 tablespoons olive oil, plus extra if needed

2 garlic cloves, crushed

handful of basil leaves

1 x 400 g (14 oz) tin peeled plum tomatoes

8 anchovy fillets preserved in oil, drained (optional)

Remove the veal escalopes from the fridge 20 minutes before cooking so they come to room temperature.

Cut the mozzarella into five or six 1 cm (½ inch) thick slices. Place on a clean tea towel or paper towel to soak up any excess moisture.

To tenderise the veal, place each escalope between two sheets of baking parchment and lightly bash five or six times with a rolling pin. Turn it 90 degrees and bash again until your slices are about 5 mm (¼ inch) thick.

Lightly season each side with salt and pepper. Tip the flour onto a wide plate, then dip each escalope into the flour, making sure they are evenly coated on both sides, then transfer to another plate, shaking off any excess flour as you go.

Place the butter in a wide frying pan with a tight-fitting lid over a medium heat until melted and sizzling. Add as many escalopes as will fit comfortably in one layer and cook on each side for 1 minute or so until they are sealed and have a little colour. Lift out with tongs and return them to the plate, then repeat with a second batch of veal if necessary, adding a little more butter or oil if the pan looks dry.

Use a wooden spoon to lift any bits caught on the bottom of the pan so they don't burn. Add the olive oil, garlic and basil leaves and leave to infuse for a minute or so. Add the tomatoes, breaking them up with the end of your spoon. Half-fill the empty tin with water and swish it around to pick up any remaining tomato and pour the tomatoey water into the pan. Add a generous pinch of salt and leave to bubble away over medium heat for 10 minutes, stirring occasionally and continuing to break up any large bits of tomato with the spoon.

Return the veal to the pan, spoon over some of the sauce and simmer for 3 minutes. Using tongs, turn the escalopes over and drape two anchovy fillets over each piece (if using), followed by the mozzarella slices and a grind of black pepper. Cover and cook for 5 minutes or until the mozzarella has melted.

Remove the lid, garnish with basil leaves and serve straight from the pan. Be sure to spoon lots of tomato sauce over the meat and mozzarella.

VARIATION

CHICKEN ALLA PIZZAIOLA:– Slice 2 chicken breasts in half widthways, then tenderise as described in the method until each chicken piece is about 1 cm (½ inch) thick. Season and flour the chicken, then brown for 2–3 minutes on each side. When you return it to the sauce, cook it for 5 minutes before adding the mozzarella to make sure it's completely cooked through.

DELICIOUS WITH:– Crispy new potatoes with capers or Hasselback 'hedgehog' potatoes; Grilled zucchini with garlic and chilli; Neapolitan vinegary fried zucchini and Green salad with olive oil and white wine vinegar (see pages 187, 188, 186, 184 and 174).

CHICKEN WITH CAPERS, LEMON, CHILLIES AND THYME

This citrusy chicken recipe is inspired by the flavours I most associate with southern Italy: lemons, chillies, capers and thyme. I like using drumsticks and thighs as these 'bone-in' cuts give so much flavour, and, once cooked, you can serve the chicken straight from the pan without needing to do any carving. If you have time, it really is worth marinating the chicken in the fridge overnight as the flavours will be deep and well developed, yielding the tastiest chicken possible.

PREPARATION:– 20 minutes, plus soaking and marinating time
COOKING:– 1 hour

SERVES 6

3 tablespoons salted or brined capers

6 organic chicken drumsticks, skin on

6 organic chicken thighs, skin on

grated zest and juice of 2 lemons

100 ml (3½ fl oz) olive oil

1 generous bunch of thyme, leaves picked

2 long red chillies, deseeded and finely chopped

6 garlic cloves, peeled and cut in half lengthways

3 lemons, sliced into discs

250 ml (8½ fl oz) white wine

If you are using salted capers, soak them for about 2 hours, changing the water three times. If you don't have time, use brined capers.

Prepare the chicken by trimming off any excess skin, then place the pieces in a shallow dish. Add the lemon zest and juice, 50 ml (1¾ fl oz) olive oil, thyme, chilli, garlic and 1 tablespoon capers and toss to combine. Cover and leave the marinate in the fridge for at least 2 hours or overnight.

Preheat the oven to 180°C (350°F) fan-forced.

Drizzle 2 tablespoons of olive oil into an ovenproof frying pan. Working in batches so you don't overcrowd the pan, take the chicken pieces out of the marinade, shaking to remove any excess liquid, and then lightly dab with paper towel. Add to the pan and brown on all sides, using tongs to turn the pieces as they brown. As the fat from the chicken begins to melt it can spit, so be careful. As you finish each batch, return the browned chicken to the marinade.

Use a spoon to remove any excess fat from the pan until you're just left with a slick of oil.

Lay the lemon slices and a tablespoon of capers over the bottom of the pan and place the pieces of chicken neatly on top, ideally in one packed layer. Pour over the marinade juices and the wine, and scatter over the remaining capers.

Roast for 20 minutes, then remove from the oven. Carefully tip the pan to one side and, using a serving spoon, scoop up some of the juices and pour them back over the chicken. Roast for another 25 minutes until the chicken is browned and cooked through. Rest for 5 minutes, then serve with all the delicious cooking juices and your choice of sides.

DELICIOUS WITH:– Garlicky grilled tomatoes; Neapolitan vinegary fried zucchini; Hasselback 'hedgehog' potatoes and Crispy new potatoes with capers (see pages 176, 184, 188 and 187).

Braciole di maiale al pistacchio

PISTACHIO PORK CHOPS

Go into any butcher's shop on Salina and you will find an array of pre-prepared meat dishes encrusted with Sicily's famous almonds or pistachios. The counter is lined with beautiful almond, caper and beef meatballs, or skewers of pork filled with capers and pistachios encased in a bright-green pistachio crust. I have recreated these in a slightly simpler way here using pork chops. The subtle nuttiness of pistachios pairs well with pork's mellow flavour, and it's an impressive looking dish that's easy to throw together.

PREPARATION:– 10 minutes, plus standing time
COOKING:– 15 minutes

SERVES 4

4 pork chops on the bone

sea salt and freshly ground black pepper

75 g (2¾ oz) '00' flour

1 large organic egg

150 g (5½ oz) shelled unsalted pistachios, roughly chopped

20 g (¾ oz) unsalted butter

20 ml (¾ fl oz) olive oil

1 lemon cut into wedges, to serve

At least 15 minutes before cooking, remove the pork chops from the fridge and season well with salt and pepper. If your chops still have the rind on them, cut this away, leaving about 5 mm (¼ inch) of fat. Set aside on a plate lined with paper towel and allow to come to room temperature.

Preheat the oven to 180°C (350°F) fan-forced. Line a large roasting tin with baking parchment (it needs to be big enough to fit all the chops in one layer).

Tip the flour into a wide bowl or plate and season with a pinch of salt. Beat the egg in a second wide bowl. Sprinkle the chopped pistachios onto a chopping board.

Dip one of the flat sides of each pork chop into the flour, making sure it is evenly coated. Shake off any excess flour, then dip it in the egg and coat evenly. Allow any excess to drip off, then place on the chopped pistachios, pressing down slightly to help them stick. Place in the prepared roasting tin, nutty side up, and repeat with the remaining chops. Set aside for 5 minutes so the pistachio crust settles – this will help it stay attached to the pork during cooking.

Get a wide frying pan, large enough to hold two of the chops at once. Add the butter and olive oil and heat over a medium–high heat until the butter has melted and is starting to sizzle. Increase the heat to high, add two of the chops, pistachio side up, and cook for 4 minutes to ensure the bottom gets some nice colour (you want to do this over a high heat so that it doesn't dry out). Using tongs gently turn the chops over and cook for 1 minute, making sure that the pistachios don't burn.

Transfer the chops, pistachio side up, to the roasting tin and repeat with the remaining chops. Pour over any buttery oil left in the pan and season with salt and pepper, then place in the oven for 5 minutes. Remove and rest for 10 minutes, then serve with lemon wedges, green salad and your choice of sides.

DELICIOUS WITH:–
Crispy new potatoes with capers; Grilled zucchini with garlic and chilli, and Garlicky grilled tomatoes (see pages 187, 186 and 176).

CONTORNI

SIDES

I usually like vegetables to be the centrepiece of a meal, but if they must play second fiddle to meat or fish they should still make their presence felt. The recipes in this chapter take humble ingredients and give them an extra something without overwhelming the palate. They are versatile, easy to make and pair well with lots of different dishes.

Garlicky spicy tomatoes, designed to bring out the best of a beef tomato, go equally well with whole roast sea bream or beef carpaccio as with pasta with aubergine and flaked almonds. A simple green salad dressed in nothing but olive oil, salt and white wine vinegar will cut through many a greedy cheese-laden dish, such as zucchini and basil omelette. Potatoes of course deserve a place in this chapter and I have included three of my favourite ways to eat them, all inspired by Tyrrhenian flavours or cooking methods. Grilled vegetables are the greatest staple of the coast and no matter what you order from the 'Secondi' section of the menu it will invariably come with a plate of a grilled zucchini and aubergine. I also celebrate the versatility of vegetables by suggesting a few ways dishes from the 'vegetable patch' chapter can be tweaked to make a great side for whatever main you happen to be serving.

GREEN SALAD WITH OLIVE OIL AND WHITE WINE VINEGAR

This simple 'dressed salad' is found on most menus in Tuscany and along the coast. It's one of my favourites as it's crisp, tangy and allows the lettuce to sing.

PREPARATION:– 5 minutes

SERVES 4

50 ml (1¾ fl oz) good-quality olive oil

1 tablespoon white wine vinegar

½ teaspoon sea salt

2 little gem lettuces, rinsed and dried

2 ruby gem (or red) lettuces, rinsed and dried

Whisk together the olive oil, vinegar and salt in a small bowl or jug.

Chop the lettuces crossways into 3 cm (1¼ inch) thick ribbons, discarding the bottom stalk. Transfer to a salad bowl. (You can prepare the lettuce up to an hour before dressing.)

When you're ready to serve, pour over the dressing and toss vigorously. Eat immediately.

VARIATION

WITH PEARS AND WALNUTS:–
Peel and core 2 pears and cut into 2 cm (¾ inch) thick slices. Toss in a bowl with the juice of ½ lemon so the pear doesn't brown. Roughly chop 75 g (2¾ oz) walnuts, add to the salad and toss. Eat immediately.

DELICIOUS WITH:– Pistachio pork chops; Chicken with capers, lemon, chillies and thyme; Whole sea bream cooked 'in parcels' with lemon, thyme and olives; A very thin zucchini and basil omelette and Spring vegetable stew with crostini and prosciutto dolce (see pages 168, 167, 140, 69 and 72).

CHICKPEA, CHERRY TOMATO, CUCUMBER AND MINT SALAD

Chickpeas are a stalwart of Italian agriculture, and in Italy you can get delicious 'ceci giganti' (giant chickpeas), which are becoming more widely available elsewhere in the world. I love the colours of this substantial salad, which sits beautifully alongside an array of vegetarian dishes or simply on its own on a hot summer's day.

PREPARATION:– 15 minutes, plus standing time

SERVES 6

1 red onion, cut in half and sliced into half moons

200 g (7 oz) cherry tomatoes, sliced into quarters

½ cucumber (about 150 g/ 5½ oz), sliced into pieces a similar size to the tomato quarters

200 g (7 oz) giant chickpeas from a jar

large handful each of mint, basil and flat-leaf parsley leaves, roughly chopped

3 tablespoons olive oil

juice of ½ lemon

sea salt and freshly ground black pepper

Put the onion in a shallow bowl, cover with cold water and leave to soak for at least 15 minutes or up to an hour to soften and mellow the flavour.

Place the tomato and cucumber in a salad bowl large enough for all the ingredients.

Drain the chickpeas in a colander over the sink, then rinse under cold running water. Leave for a minute to drain off all excess water, then transfer to the salad bowl. You can pre-prepare the salad to this point and set aside for up to an hour.

Drain the onion and add to the salad, along with the chopped herbs. Add the olive oil and lemon juice, season well with salt and pepper and toss to coat and combine. Serve immediately.

DELICIOUS WITH:– As a starter before Calamarata pasta with aubergine, olives, pecorino romano and almonds or with Grilled zucchini with garlic and chilli (see pages 92 and 186).

GARLICKY GRILLED TOMATOES

I am always looking for a way to get the most out of bland supermarket tomatoes and this dish is it. It looks beautiful and somehow elevates a boring beef tomato into something rich, sweet and full of flavour. It's based on a recipe by the great Yotam Ottolenghi but, while his dish features Middle Eastern spices, my version is inspired by the key flavours of the Tyrrhenian: garlic, chilli and oregano.

PREPARATION:– 15 minutes, plus standing time
COOKING:– 25 minutes

SERVES 6

100 ml (3½ fl oz) olive oil

2 mild long red chillies, deseeded and finely sliced

½ teaspoon chilli flakes

10 garlic cloves, finely sliced lengthways

2 teaspoons dried oregano

handful of flat-leaf parsley sprigs, leaves and stalks separated

4 beef tomatoes, sliced crossways into 5 mm (¼ inch) thick discs

1 teaspoon fine sea salt

Put the olive oil, fresh and dried chilli, garlic and oregano in a small saucepan and gently cook over a medium heat for 5 minutes, allowing the flavours to infuse the oil. Reduce the heat, add the parsley stalks and cook for another 5 minutes, being careful not to let the garlic get too brown – it should be golden and sticky. Remove from the heat for a minute or so if you're worried it's getting too dark.

Set the pan aside for 10 minutes while you prepare the tomatoes.

Preheat the oven grill to 200°C (400°F) fan-forced.

Place the tomato discs in a roasting tin large enough to accommodate them in one layer. Dip a pastry brush into the garlicky spicy oil and brush liberally over the tomatoes. Don't use it all as you'll need the rest later. Sprinkle the tomatoes evenly with the salt. Put the tin on the highest shelf of the oven and grill for 15 minutes.

Remove from the oven and leave until cool enough to handle, then use a spatula to transfer the tomatoes to a wide serving plate. Spoon over the garlic, chilli and herbs and drizzle with the remaining infused oil.

Set aside to cool while you prepare the rest of your meal. Serve slightly warm or at room temperature.

DELICIOUS WITH:– Baked sea bream with almond flakes; Sea bass with pistachios, pine nuts and sun-dried tomatoes; Whole sea bream cooked 'in parcels' with lemon, thyme and olives; Chicken with capers, lemon, chillies and thyme, and steamed zucchini with lemon (see pages 142, 145, 140, 167 and 23).

SALINA AND THE AEOLIAN ISLANDS

 The Aeolian Islands are not easy to get to. To reach this mystical cluster of seven volcanic rocks dashed across the Tyrrhenian Sea just north of Sicily, first you must travel to Palermo, Milazzo or even Naples, before catching a ferry or high-speed hydrofoil. From wherever you are in Europe, it will take at least a day. It requires commitment, and you will only feel the *Odyssey*-like journey was worth it when the hydrofoil finally pulls into the port of Santa Marina Salina. I have a vivid memory of the first time I disembarked in this pretty, unassuming port, lapped by a sparkling cobalt sea and hugged by a warm almond-scented breeze. All my travel weariness evaporated and I knew that lazy days of swimming, eating and perhaps the occasional gentle stroll lay ahead.

Santa Marina is the largest town on Salina, the second largest of the Aeolian Islands. They all have romantic names laden with history and mythology: Vulcano, Lipari, Panarea, Stromboli and the two most remote – Alicudi and Filicudi. If you look out towards them from Sicily, they seem like a mysterious apparition and the day's visibility will determine how clearly they can be glimpsed. Their remoteness is a large part of why the authentic charm and sleepy calm that envelop the archipelago have survived despite the onslaught of mass tourism.

My first visit was in May 2017. I had long been obsessed by the idea of the Aeolians after seeing them in Rossellini's neoclassic *Stromboli* with Ingrid Bergman (1950) and the charming *Il Postino* (1992), which depicts the Chilean poet Pablo Neruda's exile on Salina. But perhaps the most thrilling association for me was Giuseppe Tomasi di Lampedusa's novel *The Leopard*, his leading character Don Fabrizio having been the Prince of Salina.

We arrived extremely early in the season before most of the tourists. The bougainvillea was in full bloom and I was blown away by the natural beauty, though slightly unnerved by the eerie quiet. We took a taxi north to the town of Malfa – eccentrically one of three municipalities on this tiny island – and found the only bar that was open, Bar Malvasia, named after the sweet wine the Aeolians are famous for. We tentatively asked if we could order some lunch. They looked at us in surprise, as though they hadn't quite been expecting any non-island dwellers just yet and I wondered if we'd made a blunder coming so early in the season. Minutes later a perfect caponata appeared, made with the island's most famous export, capers. At exactly 3.30 pm, as though lunchtime siestas were timed to the minute, people began to appear, descending sleepily from their homes to crack on with the business of the afternoon. My mood instantly lifted and a profound tranquillity enveloped us as we set about enjoying the flavours, aromas and beauty of the island. It isn't just the natural beauty that pulls me back to Salina every year. The island combines the best of Southern Italy and Sicily: laidback glamour, faded grandeur, pink-plastered churches, delicious food and a vague aura of chaos.

At its centre there are two extinct volcanos, which rise up as twin peaks, dominating the landscape. The lower one is called Monte dei Porri (Mountain of the Leeks), while Monte Fossa delle Felci is the highest point in all the Aeolians, rising to 962 metres (3156 feet). These mountains provide great hiking in cooler months and are revered by locals. The seeming calm of the Aeolians masks a dramatic relationship with nature. Life on the islands is hard for months of the year, with periods of ferocious heat in summer and buffeting winds and storms in winter. Vulcano and Stromboli are still volcanically active, Stromboli in particular bubbles away, gently erupting most evenings, with more dramatic, dangerous eruptions taking place every couple of years. The Roman myths surrounding the islands reflect their elemental energy; it is said that Vulcan, son of Jupiter and God of volcanoes, had his metal workshop under the Aeolian island he gave his name to (Vulcano), now a popular holiday destination for anyone who fancies a rather smelly sulphuric mud bath. Lipari is the largest and most inhabited of the Aeolians, boasting a proper hospital and year-round infrastructure. It was named after the god Liparus, whose daughter Cyane married Aeolus, the ruler of winds and master of navigation. His face and full cheeks, puffing furiously, appear everywhere, from terracotta pots to the piazza in front of the church of Malfa, which is tiled with a wind compass to indicate the direction the wind is blowing. There are three winds that elicit the most complaints from inhabitants: 'Tramontana', a prevalent wind along the west coast of Italy that brings cool air down from the Alps and makes the sea very choppy for boats; the north-westerly 'Mistral', famed in the South of France for causing madness; and the south-easterly 'Scirocco' which sweeps up from Africa, bringing with it the hot, dusty air from the Sahara. The Scirocco induces foul tempers as everyone feels like they have a giant hairdryer pointed at them.

Aeolus was said to keep the winds at bay in the many caves on the islands, and in Homer's *Odyssey* he had an encounter with Odysseus on his long journey home to Ithaka. After Odysseus's adventure with the cyclops Polyphemus, he and his men arrived on Lipari, asking for refuge and respite. Aeolus welcomed them and they stayed for a month, at the end of which Odysseus appealed to his new friend for help getting home. Aeolus agreed and presented Odysseus with an ox-hide bag containing all but the westerly wind, so that any storms that might upset the journey were trapped in the bag, ensuring a calm and safe passage home. Aeolus gave strict instructions that on no account should the bag be opened, and Odysseus guarded it night and day, not sleeping for ten days. As the journey was coming to an end and Ithaka was in sight, overcome with exhaustion, Odysseus fell asleep. Suspecting that he was hiding some sort of treasure and keen to share the spoils, the crew opened the bag and were immediately blown back from Ithaka to the Aeolians, where a furious Aeolus left Odysseus to continue the lengthy journey home unaided.

The food of the Aeolians is defined by the islands' insularity. Being so remote, inhabitants historically had to rely on what the land and sea could provide, though the many passing traders and invaders brought with them culinary traditions that have been incorporated into the local cuisine. Over the course of centuries Byzantines, Arabs, Normans, French and Spanish all added flavours and fragrances to the islands' gastronomy. With the Greeks came honey and salted ricotta; the Arabs introduced oranges, lemons, rice, jasmine, aubergines and sugar, which began to replace honey in the preparation of many sweet dishes. Importantly they also brought sherbets, the precursor to the famous Sicilian and Aeolian granita.

Vegetables love volcanic soil, and many of my favourites thrive here: asparagus, wild fennel, broad beans, onions, zucchini, potatoes, aubergine, peppers, tomatoes and of course capers – all produce with which I can quickly rustle up something delicious. Every inch of land on the islands has always been heavily farmed – you can still see the many terraces for vineyards and vegetables. Livestock is limited to goats, pigs, rabbits and chickens, but the sea has always been most plentiful, offering tuna, sea bass, swordfish and the famous totano (squid), which is cooked in a variety of ways throughout the island. Ancient Greek historian Diodorus of Sicily expressly wrote that the sea of Lipari 'provided its inhabitants with fish of every variety and in huge quantities'. He also referred to the fertility of the island: 'rich of those fruits which offer huge pleasure to those who enjoy them'. This is also illustrated by the archaeological remains discovered throughout the Aeolians, which prove that islanders have been growing grapes and producing wine for over 4000 years.

In June 2022 our lovely friend, a boatman named Samuele, took us to Filicudi, where there is a Neolithic citadel perched atop the mountain. Recent archaeological digs have found that there are settlements on Filicudi and Salina dating back to the Bronze Age. More recently, invasions by pirates such as the Ottoman admiral Barbarossa (who exported all the inhabitants of Salina as slaves) led to the island being repopulated in the mid-16th century by people from Venice and Amalfi. Later on, the Spanish Bourbon era brought with it tomatoes, peppers, potatoes and cacao. On the way home from Filicudi, Samuele spotted a couple of seagulls flapping furiously in the middle of the sea. He diverted the boat over to the commotion and, in an act of great bravery (or treachery), snatched a beautiful squid out of the seagull's beak. The squid was gushing jet-black ink, but once Samuele had expertly washed it and gutted it, he handed us this perfect white piece of flesh to take home for supper.

In the early 20th century, between the wars, the islands suffered a huge economic crisis and could no longer rely on the exports of their wines, fish and capers to support them. There was a mass migration exodus, with 70 per cent of the island's population emigrating to Australia. It is not something many islanders talk about today. In fact, it was only by chatting to some dear friends in Venice about my love of Salina that I discovered the husband – a tall, blonde Australian – was not just from Salina, but from my favourite town of Malfa through both his sets of grandparents.

Nowadays, the islands' economies have recovered through tourism and a revival in exports of local produce (I know one caper farmer whose best customer is a shop in Tokyo). Aside from sweet Malvasia wine, drunk by locals at all times of day in little stemmed glasses, one modest ingredient embodies Aeolian, and particularly Salinian, cooking: capers. They are cooked in antipasti, salads, pasta, with fish, meat and even served simply on toast or candied on desserts (see Caponata with buffalo mozzarella on page 81). The insularity of the Aeolians does make culinary offerings a little limited. Anyone staying for a prolonged period may suddenly hanker for something that doesn't feature almonds, capers or lemons – I have one friend who after two weeks on Filicudi said she could never look at a totano again – but this is what I like about Aeolian cuisine. It makes the most of what is offered by the land and sea because it has always had to. In an age of everything being available everywhere all the time, sometimes it's comforting to be forced to make do with a limited palate.

Zucchine alla scapece

NEAPOLITAN VINEGARY FRIED ZUCCHINI

The origins of this traditional Neapolitan recipe reach back to when Naples was under Spanish rule. 'Scapace' is likely derived from the Spanish 'escabeche', which in cooking terms means to marinate in vinegar, although some say that this dish dates all the way back to Ancient Rome. It's a lovely aromatic side dish, easy to execute, but long in its preparation as the zucchini discs need to be drained of their water (by salting in a colander or, in old Italian tradition, being left out in the blazing sun for a few hours). The discs are then fried and marinated in the vinegar dressing for at least an hour, or overnight. The result is well worth it as the hands-on time is minimal and the flavour return is high – it's fabulous with fish and meat.

PREPARATION:– 15 minutes, plus standing and marinating time
COOKING:– 10 minutes

SERVES 6

1 kg (2 lb 3 oz) zucchini, sliced into thin discs

sea salt and freshly ground black pepper

80 ml (2½ fl oz) olive oil

25 ml (¾ fl oz) white wine vinegar

2 garlic cloves, crushed

grated zest and juice of 1 lemon

sea salt and freshly ground black pepper

handful of mint leaves, finely chopped, reserve a few whole leaves to garnish

Toss the zucchini with lots of salt, then place in a colander over the sink and leave for 1 hour to drain off any excess moisture. Rinse under cold running water and pat dry with a clean tea towel or paper towel.

Heat half the olive oil in a large frying pan over a medium heat. Working in batches, add the zucchini slices and fry until brown on both sides, turning to make sure they are evenly cooked. Transfer to a large plate lined with paper towel to drain.

Pour the remaining olive oil into a small jug, add the remaining ingredients and whisk with a fork to combine.

Arrange a layer of zucchini on a serving dish and pour over some of the dressing. Repeat until you have laid out all the zucchini and used all the dressing, then leave to marinate for 1 hour. Toss over extra mint leaves and serve at room temperature.

DELICIOUS WITH:– Sea bass with pistachios; pine nuts and sun-dried tomatoes; Baked sea bream with almond flakes; Whole sea bream cooked 'in parcels' with lemon, thyme and olives, and Chicken with capers, lemon, chillies and thyme (see pages 145, 142, 140 and 167).

GRILLED ZUCCHINI WITH GARLIC AND CHILLI

Along with charred discs of aubergine, grilled zucchini is the stalwart of Italian coastal side dishes. No matter where you are or what you order, the offered accompaniment will almost always be 'verdure grigliata' (grilled vegetables). The beauty of barbecuing or grilling vegetables is that you don't need any oil, so they are light as well as flavourful. You can also prepare them a few hours ahead of time and serve at room temperature, which is very convenient indeed. In short, they are perfect: simple, easy to execute and not too rich.

PREPARATION:– 10 minutes
COOKING:– 15 minutes

SERVES 6

3 large zucchini

3 tablespoons olive oil

juice of ½ lemon

sea salt and freshly ground black pepper

1 garlic clove, finely chopped

1 mild red chilli, deseeded and finely chopped

Slice the zucchini lengthways into even 1 cm (½ inch) thick strips. If your knife wobbles and you cut some uneven slices, don't worry – you can hide them underneath their prettier counterparts when you lay them out.

Heat a chargrill pan over a high heat until it's piping hot. When you can feel heat radiating from it, add as many strips as will fit in one layer (you'll need to do this in batches so be patient). Grill for about 3 minutes, then lift up the slices with a pair of tongs and check the underside – you want to see deep black stripes etched into the bottom. Flip them over and cook for another 2–3 minutes until suitably blackened and a little charred, then transfer to a plate. Repeat with the remaining zucchini.

Arrange the grilled strips on a serving dish. Drizzle over the olive oil, a squeeze of lemon and some salt and pepper. Scatter over the garlic and chilli and serve.

NOTE:– Pictured on page 28

VARIATIONS

AUBERGINE:– This works just as well with aubergine – prepare and grill it in exactly the same way.

WITH MOZZARELLA:– Serve with a ball of buffalo mozzarella for a delicious vegetarian main.

DELICIOUS WITH:– Chicken with capers, lemon, chillies and thyme; Whole sea bream cooked 'in parcels' with lemon, thyme and olives; Baked sea bream with almond flakes; Caponata with buffalo mozzarella; Roast peppers with salsa verde and burrata (see pages 167, 140, 142, 81 and 70).

Patate novelle croccanti con capperi

CRISPY NEW POTATOES WITH CAPERS

I love potatoes and enjoy thinking up ways to cook them that don't involve rosemary (my usual go to when flavouring potatoes). Good-quality salted capers, restored to their delicious plumpness after soaking in water, add a wonderful aromatic piquancy, which, when paired with the lemon zest, really livens them up. Parboiling the potatoes and leaving them to cool before shallow-frying them with the garlic and capers ensures that you have a nicely cooked interior with a lovely crisp layer on the outside. This is a really easy side dish which goes very well with meat, fish or any vegetarian main.

PREPARATION:– 10 minutes, plus soaking and cooling time
COOKING:– 25 minutes

SERVES 6

600 g (1 lb 5 oz) new potatoes, sliced in half lengthways

40 ml (1¼ fl oz) olive oil

1 garlic clove, peeled and squashed with the edge of a knife

sea salt

100 g (3½ oz) salted capers, rinsed and soaked in water for at least 2 hours

grated zest of 1 lemon

Bring a saucepan of salted water to the boil over a high heat, add the potatoes and parboil for 7–10 minutes. Drain and leave to cool for 15 minutes.

Pour the olive oil into a wide frying pan, large enough to accommodate the potatoes. Add the garlic and a generous pinch of salt and heat over a medium heat until the garlic is sizzling.

Add the potatoes and another good pinch of salt, and toss well to make sure they are all evenly coated in oil. Cook for 5 minutes. Add the capers and, using tongs, turn the potatoes over to make sure they cook and brown evenly. The first side should have a lovely golden-brown colour. Cook for another 10 minutes, tossing or turning the potatoes occasionally.

Sprinkle over the lemon zest and serve immediately.

NOTE:– Pictured on page 169

DELICIOUS WITH:– Pistachio pork chops; Veal escalopes in tomato sauce with mozzarella and anchovy; Grilled tuna steaks with fresh peas and salsa verde; Baked sea bream with almond flakes, and Roast peppers with salsa verde and burrata (see pages 168, 164, 139, 142 and 70).

HASSELBACK 'HEDGEHOG' POTATOES

Not strictly an Italian way of preparing potatoes, but one I have become fond of for its simplicity and visual charm. I've called these 'hedgehog' potatoes as the slits across the back remind me in an abstract way of the hedgehogs and porcupines that I've seen all my life in Tuscany. It's a great recipe because after you have made the cuts across the potatoes, you stick them in the oven and an hour later have a delicious and impressive side dish.

PREPARATION:– 15 minutes
COOKING:– 45 minutes

SERVES 6

4 tablespoons olive oil

fine sea salt

4 rosemary sprigs, cut into thirds

1.5 kg (3 lb 5 oz) medium floury potatoes

6 garlic cloves, peeled and squashed with the edge of a knife

flaky sea salt

Preheat the oven to 180°C (350°F) fan-forced.

Pour the olive oil into a small bowl and add a generous pinch of fine salt and one of the cut rosemary sprigs.

To prepare the potatoes, use a sharp knife to make lots of deep slits crossways a few millimetres apart. The knife should go most of the way into the potato but not right through. I find it helpful to position each potato lengthways between the handles of two wooden spoons – the handles block the knife so it doesn't cut all the way through. Repeat with the remaining potatoes.

Place the prepped potatoes in a roasting tin and gently pull apart to open the cuts. Use a pastry brush to brush the rosemary-infused olive oil over the potatoes, making sure they are generously coated and that some oil gets into the slits. Season with a little more fine salt, again making sure that some gets into the slits. Randomly wedge the rosemary sprigs into the cuts so tufts are sticking out here and there. Toss in the garlic cloves.

Roast for 45 minutes or until the potato skins are golden and the flesh is tender. (If you are using new potatoes shave about 15 minutes off the cooking time; if your potatoes are quite large you may need to cook them for another 15 minutes or so.) Transfer to a serving bowl and scatter over a little flaky salt.

DELICIOUS WITH:– Chicken with capers, lemon, chillies and thyme; Sea bass with pistachios, pine nuts and sun-dried tomatoes, and Baked cod with cherry tomatoes, lemon and capers (see pages 167, 145 and 129).

BRAISED POTATOES AND ARTICHOKES

This cosy and comforting side dish is perfect for the cooler months when round Italian artichokes typical of Lazio (Carciofo Romanesco) and Campania (Carciofo di Paestum) are at their best. It's great with fish and meat, or makes a hearty vegetarian main.

PREPARATION:– 20 minutes
COOKING:– 45 minutes

SERVES 6

½ lemon

3 Sardinian spiky or Roman mammole artichokes

30 g (1 oz) butter

3 tablespoons olive oil

1 red onion, finely chopped

sea salt and freshly ground black pepper

800 g (1 lb 12 oz) potatoes, peeled and sliced into quarters

200 ml (7 fl oz) white wine

large handful of flat-leaf parsley, leaves picked

DELICIOUS WITH:–
Baked aubergine and ricotta sformato with tomato sauce; Roast peppers with salsa verde and burrata; Chicken with capers, lemon, chillies and thyme; Pistachio pork chops; Baked sea bream with almond flakes (see pages 86, 70, 167, 168 and 142).

Squeeze the lemon juice into a bowl of cold water and drop in the lemon half. You will put your prepped artichokes in the acidulated water to stop them turning brown. Take an artichoke and tear off the rough outer leaves (the ones that feel rough in your hands, and that your digestive system is clearly not up to). Using a vegetable peeler, peel away the dark green from the stem until you reach a lighter green, the colour of fresh peas. Rub the newly exposed tender flesh with the lemon half. Cut the top off the artichoke (about 4 cm/1½ inch below the spike), then cut the prepared artichoke into quarters lengthways and remove the hairy 'choke' with a paring knife. Drop the quarters into the lemony water and repeat with the remaining artichokes.

In a wide frying pan with a tight-fitting lid, melt the butter with the olive oil over medium heat until sizzling. Add the onion and a generous pinch of salt and pepper, then cook gently for about 5 minutes until translucent.

Add the artichoke quarters (reserve the lemony water they have been sitting in) and stir to make sure they are evenly coated in oil and butter. Cook for 5 minutes, stirring occasionally. Add 2 ladlefuls of the lemony water, along with the potato, wine, half the parsley and another generous pinch of salt. Reduce the heat and simmer gently for 20–25 minutes, stirring occasionally, until the vegetables are tender and the cooking liquid has reduced a little.

Uncover the pan, increase the heat to high and cook for another 5–10 minutes to allow the liquid to reduce even further. Switch off the heat, cover and set aside until you are ready to serve. The dish is even more delicious reheated the next day. Just before serving, scatter over the remaining parsley.

THESE RECIPES CAN ALSO BE TWEAKED TO SERVE AS SIDE DISHES:–

Roast peppers with salsa verde and burrata (page 70):– **serve without the burrata**

Caponata with buffalo mozzarella (page 81):– **serve without the mozzarella and bread**

Maurizia's potato, olive and caper salad (page 84)

DOLCI

SWEETS

DOLCI

 As you head south of Tuscany the desserts become decidedly greedier and more imaginative the further down the boot of Italy you go. Tuscany is not known for its patisserie, which veers into spartan territory at times, but Campania and Sicily can lay claim to the country's most exciting sweets. As the main produce of Tuscany was historically wine and olive oil, these were mixed with seasonal fruit to bake simple cakes or dry biscuits such as ciambelline al vino or, as we were given for a mid-afternoon snack when I was in elementary school, stale pane toscano (local unsalted bread) sprinkled with sugar and drizzled with red wine.

Further down the coast things become less parsimonious and more exciting, and in Lazio they have a plethora of ways to cook one of their most abundant fruits – cherries. In my view, the simplest and most delicious is in a summery cherry tart. Heavily influenced by the patisseries of the French court during the Bourbon reign, Naples and the Amalfi Coast are famed for beautiful and hugely complex pastries. The classic sfogliatella is one I feel happy to leave to the master Neapolitan patissiers, but I do often make a shortcrust pastry version that is decidedly more achievable. Lemons are the flavour of the day in Campania, and are used to flavour cream, sponges, whipped ricotta and nutty torte al caprese. Of course, as a historically poor region Campania also had its puddings born of necessity, such as zeppole (leftover dough deep-fried and dressed in syrup or sugar). A version of this dates back to when the area was run by the Greeks, who would make honey and rosemary-soaked fritters along the coast of Cilento. Hop over the water to Sicily and you'll find yourself in the Italian capital of the sweet tooth.

The Arabs were the first to bring sugarcane to Sicily and they have been perfecting their sweet dishes ever since, with a particular proficiency for mixing them with the island's bounty of nuts: pistachios and almonds. A visit to a Sicilian bar or bakery is a pleasurable assault on the senses – colourful layered pastries and sculpted marzipan shine like jewels as they are often covered with candied fruit. Breakfast is a particularly rich affair, as sweet pistachio cream in all its forms is offered up with your morning coffee in croissants filled with pistachio cream or in plain, fluffy brioche buns filled with pistachio ice cream. Not having the constitution of a Sicilian, this breakfast is one I can only enjoy when I have absolutely nothing to do aside from lie on a sunbed as it sends me straight to sleep.

In picking and reinterpreting sweet recipes from the Tyrrhenian coast, I have chosen recipes that are achievable in a home kitchen and have tried to ensure they offer at least one, maybe two, but preferably all three of the following attributes: fresh, fruity or creamy. These are the words that always come to me when I am in a gloriously greedy Campanian or Sicilian cafe.

BLACKBERRY GRANITA

Granita is a chilled Sicilian sweet treat, designed to counter the ferocious heat when richer desserts prove too much even for the famously sweet-toothed locals. Granitas are served to finish off a meal, or for elevenses, or at tea time, or at any point in the day really. They are typically kept churning in machines to maintain a loose consistency that can be easily eaten with a spoon. On Salina, there is a famous granita outlet called Da Alfredo at Lingua (pictured opposite), looking towards the island of Lipari. A visit there on your scooter for a tall glass of granita di gelsi neri (mulberry) or al pistachio is a must. Even without an ice-cream machine, granita is surprisingly easy to make. Sicilians often top their granitas with whipped cream and chopped nuts, or enjoy it plain with a fresh fruit garnish. Mulberries are tricky to find outside Sicily so I have adapted this recipe to use blackberries, but it works equally well with blueberries, cherries or raspberries. Use frozen fruit if you can't find any fresh.

PREPARATION:– 15 minutes, plus cooling and freezing time
COOKING:– 15 minutes

SERVES 6

500 g (1 lb 2 oz) fresh or frozen blackberries

120 g (4½ oz) caster sugar

juice of 1 lemon, plus extra if needed

double cream or Pistachio granita (see page 201), to serve (optional)

Combine the berries and 100 ml (3½ fl oz) water in a medium saucepan and place over a medium heat. Leave for about 10 minutes, before mixing with a spoon to check the blackberries are well softened. Allow to cool slightly, then lightly whizz with a handheld blender to a thick, dark pulp – it's important not to overdo it or the bitter seeds will be blitzed into the pulp and be almost impossible to separate. When the pulp is no longer piping hot, pass it through a fine mesh sieve into a bowl to separate the pulp and juice from the skin and seeds. This should yield about 400 ml (13½ fl oz) blackberry pulp. Set aside while you make the sugar syrup.

Fill the saucepan you used for the blackberries with 500 ml (17 fl oz) water and add the sugar, stirring to encourage it to dissolve. Bring to the boil over a medium heat, swirling the pan occasionally. As soon as it starts bubbling, remove the syrup from the heat so it doesn't begin to caramelise. Stir in the strained blackberry pulp and lemon juice. Give it a quick taste – if it's too sweet add a squeeze more lemon juice. The sweetness will depend on the ripeness of your berries or if you are using frozen. When you're happy with the flavour, set the mixture aside to cool completely.

Pour into a shallow container or roasting tin that will fit in the freezer and freeze for 2 hours. Use a sturdy fork to scrape and agitate the parts of the pulp that are freezing; this will help the crystals to freeze in smaller, more homogenous pieces rather than one big block. Return to the freezer for a minimum of 3 hours, scraping the granita every hour or so.

About 10 minutes before serving, take the granita out of the freezer to soften. Spoon into individual glasses and serve as is, or top with double cream or a scoop of pistachio granita.

Granita al limone

LEMON GRANITA

This icy lemony dessert is perfect for rounding off a rich meal on a hot summer's day. It's also ideal as a pre-dinner drink with a drop of beer – see Beer and lemon granita shandy (page 46). You can pre-make the lemon granita and leave it in the freezer for up to two weeks.

PREPARATION:– 20 minutes, plus cooling and freezing time
COOKING:– 5 minutes

SERVES 6

8 unwaxed lemons (if you can find the large kind with leaves from Amalfi all the better)

250 g (9 oz) caster sugar

mint leaves, to garnish

Finely grate the zest of five lemons and set aside in a bowl. Juice all eight lemons.

Combine the sugar, lemon zest and 400 ml (13½ fl oz) water in a small saucepan and stir over a medium heat with a wooden spoon to encourage the sugar to dissolve. As soon as the lemony sugar syrup comes to the boil, switch off the heat and set aside for about 30 minutes to infuse and cool completely.

Meanwhile, pass the lemon juice through a fine mesh strainer to remove any pulp and stray pips. Stir the strained juice into the sugar syrup, then pour into a shallow container or roasting tin that will fit in the freezer. Place in the fridge for an hour to steep, then transfer to the freezer, making sure it is level. It will take about 5 hours to achieve the light, airy granita texture we're after. Set an alarm for every hour or so and use a sturdy fork to scrape and agitate the parts that are freezing; this will help the crystals to freeze in smaller, more homogenous pieces rather than one big block.

About 10 minutes before serving, take the granita out of the freezer to soften. Spoon into individual cocktail glasses and top with a few mint leaves.

VARIATION

A BOOZY PUDDING:– Spoon the granita into glasses and pour over a shot of homemade limoncello (see page 232) or vodka.

PISTACHIO GRANITA

Granita is said to have been invented at the top of Mount Etna as a way of flavouring the snow and ice at those heights. Pistachio granita is the signature flavour at Da Alfredo on the island of Salina, where they are very strict about the combination of flavours you can order, insisting that you can't have two different flavours if 'non si lega bene' (they don't go well). The recipe calls for the skins to be removed. This sounds laborious but it's very much worth the bother and will only take you about 15 minutes. You can skip this step if you are short on time, but the finished granita will have a slightly rougher texture with bits of papery skin in the mix. My husband prefers it like that, so really it's a matter of personal taste and time constraints.

PREPARATION:– 25 minutes, plus cooling and freezing time
COOKING:– 5 minutes

SERVES 6

300 g (10½ oz) unsalted pistachios

100 g (3½ oz) caster sugar

250 ml (8½ fl oz) unsweetened almond or oat milk

double cream or Blackberry granita (see page 198), to serve (optional)

Put the pistachios in a heatproof bowl, cover with boiling water and leave to sit for 5 minutes. Drain, then tip onto a clean tea towel. Vigorously rub the pistachios between two layers of tea towel to remove the papery skins and discard. Transfer the de-skinned pistachios to a bowl and peel away any stubborn skins from the remaining pistachios, transferring them to the bowl as you go.

Blitz half the pistachios in a food processor for 1 minute or until you have a rough texture. Add the rest and blitz again for another minute until the first batch of pistachios are finely chopped and the rest still retain some texture. Set aside while you make the sugar syrup.

Combine the sugar and 300 ml (10 fl oz) water in a small saucepan and stir over a low heat with a wooden spoon to encourage the sugar to dissolve. As soon as the sugar syrup comes to the boil, switch off the heat so it doesn't caramelise. Stir in the pistachios and milk, then set aside for about 30 minutes to infuse and cool completely.

Pour into a shallow container or roasting tin that will fit in the freezer and freeze for 2 hours. Use a sturdy fork to scrape and agitate the parts that are freezing; this will help the crystals to freeze in smaller, more homogenous pieces rather than one big block. Return to the freezer for a minimum of 3 hours, scraping the granita every hour or so (set an alarm to remind yourself).

About 10 minutes before serving, take the granita out of the freezer to soften. Spoon into individual glasses and serve as is, or top with double cream or a scoop of blackberry granita.

Panna cotta al pistacchio

PISTACHIO PANNA COTTA

Pistachio cream is a staple of the Sicilian kitchen and is used in many breakfast pastries. It is similar to chocolate spread but is (unsurprisingly) green and tastes gloriously of pistachios. You can find jars of crema di pistachio in most supermarkets in Italy, or it's widely available online. Mixing pistachio cream with panna cotta is an indulgent twist on a classic, bringing a nutty sweetness to the cream as well as acting as a second setting agent, meaning you need less gelatin. I serve these in cocktail glasses and never turn them out, mainly because their green colour doesn't look as attractive domed on a plate as it does sitting in a glass topped with chopped pistachios or a few fresh raspberries.

PREPARATION:– 10 minutes, plus soaking and chilling time
COOKING:– 5 minutes

SERVES 4

handful of unsalted pistachios, roughly chopped

handful of raspberries (optional)

PANNA COTTA

2 x 2 g (1⁄16 oz) gelatine leaves

400 ml (14 fl oz) double cream

30 g (1 oz) caster sugar

1 vanilla pod, split and seeds scraped

80 g (2¾ oz) pistachio cream

To make the panna cotta, using scissors, cut the gelatine sheets into a small bowl and cover with cold water. Leave to soak for 15 minutes or as instructed on the packet.

Meanwhile, pour the cream into a medium saucepan and add the sugar, vanilla seeds and pod. Place over a medium heat and gently warm until it almost comes to the boil, then switch off immediately.

Squeeze any excess liquid out of the soaked gelatine and stir into the hot cream until it has completely dissolved. Remove the vanilla pod, then transfer to a large bowl and mix in the pistachio cream until smooth.

Divide the panna cotta evenly among four cocktail glasses, then chill in the fridge for at least 3 hours or, better still, overnight.

When you're ready to serve, top each panna cotta with a teaspoon of roughly chopped pistachios and, if you like, a few raspberries. Serve directly from the glass.

Tiramisù al lampone

RASPBERRY TIRAMISU

Tiramisu is probably the best known of all Italian puddings, with its signature combination of coffee, cream and sponge. But across Italy you can find this creamy trifle in more unusual guises, particularly in summer when berries abound. I enjoy overhearing people in the market discussing what they plan to do with their purchases and have often heard someone say the punnet they are holding in their hand is destined for a strawberry or raspberry tiramisu: delicious, fresh and slightly unexpected. This recipe is for one large tiramisu, but you can make individual portions in glasses if you prefer (as pictured).

PREPARATION:– 30 minutes, plus standing and chilling time

SERVES 6

650 g (1 lb 7 oz)
raspberries, rinsed

juice of ½ lemon

100 ml (3½ fl oz) sweet
marsala wine

75 g (2¾ oz) caster sugar

4 organic egg yolks

500 g (1 lb 2 oz) mascarpone

3 organic egg whites

about 24 savoiardi
(ladyfinger biscuits)

Roughly slice the raspberries in half – some will disintegrate into a jamlike texture, which is fine. Place in a bowl and cover with the lemon juice, marsala and 1 tablespoon of sugar. Cover and set aside at room temperature for at least 1 hour or up to overnight in the fridge.

Using handheld electric beaters, whisk the egg yolks with the remaining sugar for 2–3 minutes until thick and pale and the sugar has dissolved. Whisk in the mascarpone and set aside.

In a clean metal bowl and with clean beaters, whisk the egg whites to form soft peaks. Be careful not to take it to stiff peaks or the tiramisu will be dry rather than creamy. Gently fold the egg whites into the mascarpone mixture to make a loose velvety cream.

By now the steeped raspberries should have released some lovely ruby juices into the wine and lemon juice. Tip them into a small colander over a wide bowl to separate the liquid from the pulp (the bowl should be large enough to dip the biscuits into). Transfer the raspberry pulp to a little bowl.

Half dip the biscuits, sugar side down, into the strained raspberry liquid. Cover the bottom of your serving dish with a layer of dipped biscuits, sugar side up, then spoon over a third of the boozy raspberry pulp, spreading it out evenly. Spoon over half the mascarpone cream, smoothing it out with a spatula or the back of a spoon. Repeat with another layer of dipped ladyfingers, half the remaining the raspberries and the rest of the mascarpone. Mix together the remaining raspberry pulp and soaking liquid and spoon over the top.

Cover and leave in the fridge for at least 4–6 hours, or overnight so the flavours and textures come together. Remove from the fridge 30 minutes before serving.

VARIATION

LEMON TIRAMISU:– Grate the zest of 5 lemons. Combine 200 ml (7 fl oz) homemade (see page 232) or shop-bought limoncello, 100 ml (3½ fl oz) water, 50 g (1¾ oz) caster sugar and 1 teaspoon of grated lemon zest in a small jug or bowl. Stir to dissolve the sugar and set aside. Make the mascarpone cream, whisking the egg yolks with 60 g (2 oz) caster sugar. Add the remaining lemon zest (reserving a little for garnish), 1 tablespoon at a time, then whisk in the mascarpone. Continue with the recipe as described, replacing the raspberry liquid with the lemon mixture. Cover the first layer of dipped biscuits with half the cream, then repeat with a second layer of biscuits and the remaining cream. Sprinkle over the reserved lemon zest, then cover and chill.

Scauratielli Cilentani

ROSEMARY AND HONEY FRITTERS

These sweet Christmas treats are derived from an Ancient Greek recipe prepared in the city of Poseidon (as it was then called) on Cilento's northern coast in the 6th and 7th centuries BCE. The city would later become known as Paestum under the Romans, and its amazingly intact ruins are well worth a visit today. Scauratielli were prepared by the Greeks during the night of the winter solstice as an offering to the gods to celebrate the return of longer days and light triumphing over dark. Their Greek origins account for the shapes – alphas and omegas.

The dough is rather like a choux, brought together over heat. Shaping the fritters is meditative when done alone or great fun when done with friends and family. They are traditionally fried, which is obviously heaven, but I also give a variation for baking them, so you can choose which you prefer. The baked version won't be as crunchy or chewy, but still fragrant and delicious. A lovely sweet note to end any meal on.

PREPARATION:– 25 minutes, plus resting and standing time
COOKING:– 50 minutes

MAKES 30

peel of 1 lemon, 1 orange and 1 mandarin (use a vegetable peeler to make strips)

1 rosemary sprig

2 tablespoons caster sugar

sea salt

75 ml (2½ fl oz) white wine

50 ml (1¾ fl oz) olive oil

250 g (9 oz) '00' flour

300 ml (10 fl oz) vegetable oil

ROSEMARY HONEY

200 g (7 oz) runny honey

1 rosemary sprig

Pour 600 ml (20½ fl oz) water into a large saucepan, add the citrus peel, rosemary, sugar and a pinch of salt and bring to the boil over a high heat. Reduce the heat and leave uncovered to simmer away for 10 minutes. Add the wine and olive oil and simmer for a further 10 minutes. Remove and discard the citrus peel and rosemary.

Turn the heat right down and start adding the flour, a few tablespoons at a time, while whisking vigorously to prevent lumps forming. Once all the flour has been incorporated and you have a thick, sticky, seemingly unmanageable dough, keep whisking over the heat for another couple of minutes, then tip out onto a lightly floured surface to cool for 10–15 minutes.

When the dough is cool enough to handle, knead it for 3–5 minutes. To do this, push the dough away from you with the heel of your palm, then use your fingers to bring it back towards you, allowing the dough to fold over itself. Keep going until you have a smooth, springy dough.

At this point you can begin to shape your scauratielli. Divide the dough in half so you can make 15 fritters of each shape. Line two baking trays (that can fit in the fridge) with baking parchment and lightly dust with flour.

For the alpha shape, take a small piece of dough (about 25 g/1 oz) and roll into a 10 cm (4 inch) log around 1 cm (½ inch) thick. Loop the two ends around so they cross over themselves and you are left with a long central hole and two small tails. Gently press down on the spot when the dough crosses over itself to secure the shape. Set aside on one of the trays and repeat to make 15 scauratielli in total.

To make the omegas, make a log as you did with the alphas. Simultaneously bring both ends of the log down and around towards you; when your thumbs meet, bring them up and away from you so that the ends cross over in the centre. Gently press down on the spot when the dough crosses over itself to secure the shape. Place on the second tray and repeat until you have 15 omega scauratielli.

Leave the scauratielli to rest at room temperature for about an hour before you cook them. (If you are preparing the scauratielli for later, shape them and place on a baking tray lined with baking parchment, then freeze. You can fry them directly from frozen.)

Meanwhile, to make the rosemary honey, put the honey and rosemary sprig in a small saucepan over a medium heat until the honey becomes completely liquid and starts to bubble a little. Remove from the heat and swirl the pan around so that the rosemary is fully submerged in the hot honey. Leave to infuse while the scauratielli rest.

Heat the vegetable oil in a deep, wide frying pan over a high heat. Check the oil is ready by dropping a small piece of dough or bread in the oil: if it sizzles it's ready; if it doesn't, give it another few minutes. Line a plate or tray with paper towel to soak up any excess oil.

Working in batches so you don't overcrowd the pan, fry the scauratielli for 1 minute, then turn over with tongs or a slotted spoon and fry for a further 30–60 seconds until golden. Drain on paper towel, then pile them up on a clean serving dish. Briefly reheat the honey over a medium heat, then pour over the fritters and toss to coat. Leave for at least 10 minutes to soak up some of the honey.

You can serve them warm or at room temperature – after a couple of hours they will be wonderfully sticky with rosemary honey.

VARIATION

BAKING THE SCAURATIELLI:– Preheat the oven to 200°C (400°F) fan-forced. Arrange the scauratielli in a single layer on two baking trays lined with baking parchment. Brush with a little beaten egg, then place in the fridge until the oven has come up to temperature. Bake for 10 minutes until lightly golden. Shortly before they are ready, reheat the honey as above. Remove the scauratielli from the oven and brush with half the infused honey, then bake for another 10 minutes until they have a little more colour. Let them cool for 5 minutes, then pile them on a serving dish and pour over the remaining honey. Let it soak in for at least 10 minutes, then serve warm.

Crostata di ciliegie fresche

SUMMERY CHERRY TART

There is always a glut of cherries on Italian market stalls during the early summer. Cherries are a luxury and therefore expensive but make a great low-fuss dessert at the end of a long lunch when simply served in a pretty bowl with a few ice cubes. Cherry tart is found on most beach shack menus in June and July, and I always order it at La Strega, the restaurant on my favourite beach in Tuscany, Ansedonia (pictured), from where you can see the border with Lazio across the bay. I love this recipe as it allows the cherries to sing. Unlike at La Strega, I bake the cherries directly in the tart case without making a jam beforehand, but they magically become jamlike anyway. Allow plenty of time for the faff of halving and pitting the cherries and for the tart to properly cool so that you get a nice thick filling. It's well worth it.

PREPARATION:– 50 minutes, plus resting and chilling time
COOKING:– 50 minutes

SERVES 8

1 kg (2 lb 3 oz) black cherries

100 g (3½ oz) caster sugar

15 g (½ oz) cornflour

2 teaspoons lemon juice

creme fraiche, to serve

PASTRY

2 organic egg yolks

2 tablespoons ice-cold water

60 g (2 oz) caster sugar

240 g (8½ oz) '00' flour

pinch of sea salt

140 g (5 oz) unsalted butter, chilled and diced

1 large organic egg, beaten

To make the pastry, use a fork to gently mix the egg yolks with the ice-cold water in a small bowl. Keep in the fridge until ready to use.

Pulse the sugar, flour and salt in a food processor until combined, then add the butter and pulse until the mixture resembles breadcrumbs. With the motor running, add the egg yolk and water mixture and blend until the dough comes together into a rough ball. Switch off as soon as this happens or you will overwork it.

Alternatively, if you don't have a food processor, put the sugar, flour and a pinch of salt in a bowl and rub in the diced butter using your fingertips. Your hands should be cool and dry for this task. Once the butter is thoroughly rubbed in with no large lumps remaining, add the egg yolk mixture and combine with a fork to form a rough ball.

Tip the dough onto a lightly floured surface and gently bring it together, kneading once or twice with your hands. Shape the dough into a ball, then flatten it into a disc. Wrap it in cling film and rest in the fridge for 20 minutes.

Meanwhile, remove the stems from the cherries and cut them in half, discarding the pips. Set aside in a large bowl in the fridge.

Preheat the oven to 180°C (350°F) fan-forced. Butter and line a 20 cm (8 inch) loose-bottomed tart tin (preferably non-stick) with baking parchment.

Lightly flour the work surface again and start rolling out the rested dough. Turn it 90 degrees after each roll to prevent it from sticking to the surface and ensure you are rolling it out evenly – ideally to a 5 mm (¼ inch) thickness.

Place the tin on the pastry and cut a disc 2 cm (¾ inch) wider than the base. Ball up the excess pastry and place in the freezer for 10 minutes so that it will be easier to handle. You will use it to make the lattice strips for the top.

Loosely fold the pastry disc around your rolling pin and transfer it to the tart tin, gently pressing it into place. Using a pastry brush, coat the bottom of the pastry case with a thin layer of beaten egg and prick all over with a fork. Put the tin in the freezer for at least 10 minutes (or the fridge for 20 minutes) until the pastry is firm to the touch – this will stop it shrinking in the oven.

Lightly flour a wide plate. Roll out the chilled excess pastry to the same thickness as the base and cut out six strips, 24 cm (9½ inch) long and 1 cm (½ inch) wide. If it's a hot day, put the plate in the freezer to cool so the strips are easier to handle when assembling the tart.

Add the sugar, cornflour and lemon juice to the bowl of cherries and mix well. Retrieve the pastry case and strips from the fridge and fill the case with the sugared cherries.

Place three of the strips over the filling, equally spaced apart. Starting at one end, about 2 cm (¾ inch) in from the edge, lift the two outer strips a quarter of the way back and place a fourth strip across them in the opposite direction. Fold the outer strips back down so the fourth strip is underneath the outer strips but over the central one. Now fold the central strip back over the strip you just added and place a fifth strip across the middle so it's going over the outer strips. Fold the middle strip back down so that it goes over the one you just added. Finally, lift the two outer strips and place the last strip in the same way as you did

the fourth one. You should now have a beautifully latticed top. Press down on the ends to secure them to the pastry case and brush lightly with the beaten egg.

Bake for 50 minutes and check the top; if it hasn't browned enough bake for another 5 minutes. The cherries will have created a lot of dark liquid, but don't worry – this will thicken as the tart cools.

Cool completely in the tin for at least an hour, then place the tart case on top of an upturned bowl and ease the side of the tin away. Transfer the tart to a plate and chill in the fridge for at least 3 hours.

This is best eaten at room temperature so take the tart out of the fridge at the start of your meal. Serve with a dollop of creme fraiche.

Torta di ricotta e pere

RICOTTA, PEAR AND HAZELNUT BISCUIT CAKE

I first tasted this during a visit to the wonderful organic buffalo farm Tenuta Vannulo near Paestum, famed for its mozzarella and ricotta. On a Sunday morning their very smart breakfast 'yogurteria' allows for great people-watching as well-dressed locals enjoy brioche filled with pistachio cream, hot orange custard made with buffalo milk or indeed balls of ice-cream. As I was wondering what to order with my coffee, out came this fabulous-looking 'cake': a thick layer of snow-white cream studded with yellow pearls of pear in a sandwich that looked like dark chocolate sponge but turned out to be crisp hazelnut biscuit. I was fascinated and ordered it immediately. What made it so special was the combination of both flavours and textures. I have since discovered that this cake is famous all along the Amalfi Coast (where it was invented), but it will always remind me of that sunny morning among the rural smells of the buffalo farm at Vannulo.

PREPARATION:– 30 minutes, plus cooling and chilling time
COOKING:– 35 minutes

butter, to grease the tin

150 g (5½ oz) blanched
hazelnuts

100 g (3½ oz) unsalted butter,
plus 1 tablespoon, extra, melted

120 g (4½ oz) golden
caster sugar

4 tablespoons '00' flour

3 organic egg whites

icing sugar, for dusting
(optional)

CREAM FILLING

3 pears, ripe but firm

juice of ½ lemon

1 vanilla pod, split and
seeds scraped

150 g (5½ oz) caster sugar

10 g (¼ oz) cornflour

500 g (1 lb 2 oz) ricotta, drained

200 ml (7 fl oz) double cream

Preheat the oven to 180°C (350°F) fan-forced. Butter two round 24 cm (9½ inch) cake tins and line with baking parchment. Alternatively, you could line two baking trays with parchment, draw on two 24 cm (9½ inch) circles and pipe the mixture into the circles.

To make a start on the filling, peel and core the pears, then cut into 2 cm (¾ inch) cubes. Place in a small saucepan and add the lemon juice, vanilla seeds (discard the pod), 100 g (3½ oz) of the sugar and just enough water to cover the pear. Cut a piece of baking parchment to fit the pan and press down gently to help the pears poach and steam. Bring to the boil over a medium heat, then reduce the heat and simmer for 5–7 minutes until tender but still with a little bite – cook for a few extra minutes if the pears are very firm. Using a slotted spoon, transfer the cooked pear to a bowl. Whisk the cornflour into the poaching liquid and boil over a high heat for a minute or so to activate the flour and thicken the syrup. Pour over the pear, then leave to cool completely while you prepare the cake.

Spread the hazelnuts out on a baking tray and toast in the oven for 5 minutes or so until they begin to smell nutty. Remove and allow to cool completely, then blitz in a food processor until roughly chopped. Set aside in a bowl.

In a large bowl, cream the butter and golden caster sugar using handheld electric beaters. Mix in the flour and chopped hazelnuts, then pour over the melted butter to loosen the mixture a little.

Whisk the egg whites until stiff peaks form, adding a tablespoon of caster sugar halfway through whisking. Using a clean metal spoon, gently fold the egg whites into the hazelnut mixture, bit by bit.

Divide the batter between the prepared tins (or pipe onto the prepared trays), smooth the surface and bake for 15–20 minutes or until they look crisp and golden. Remove from the oven and set aside to cool completely in the tins. Once they are cool, remove the cakes and carefully peel away the parchment.

To finish the filling, using handheld electric beaters or a stand mixer, whisk together the ricotta and remaining sugar until smooth and shiny, about 5 minutes. Fold in the pear and the poaching liquid. In a separate bowl whip the cream for 2–3 minutes or until smooth and cloud like, then gently fold though the ricotta and pear mixture.

Before you assemble the cake, grease the ring part of a 24 cm (9½ inch) springform tin or ring mould with butter and line with a strip of baking parchment. Put one of the cakes on a serving plate or board, then place the prepared cake ring on top, lining it up with the cake as closely as possible. Fill with the ricotta pear cream, smoothing the top evenly with a spatula or the back of a spoon. Place the second cake on top and very gently press down to sandwich together. Transfer to the fridge to chill and set for at least 3 hours or overnight.

To serve, remove the ring mould and dust the top of the cake with icing sugar, if you like. The best way to cut into the cake is gently with a serrated bread knife. The cake is delicious for one day and then the top and base will go soggy so eat within 24 hours.

Torta sfogliatella frolla con arance

RICOTTA AND CINNAMON SFOGLIATELLA PIE WITH ORANGE SALAD

This fragrant pie filled with cinnamon and orange-scented ricotta and semolina is inspired by the individual shortcrust pastries served for breakfast in Naples.

PREPARATION:– 40 minutes, plus cooling and chilling time
COOKING:– 35 minutes

SERVES 8

3 oranges (preferably blood oranges)

icing sugar, for dusting

PASTRY

4 organic egg yolks

4 tablespoons iced water

120 g (4½ oz) caster sugar

480 g (1 lb 1 oz) '00' flour

2 pinches of fine sea salt

280 g (10 oz) unsalted butter, chilled and diced

1 large organic egg, beaten

RICOTTA FILLING

50 g (1¾ oz) fine semolina

fine sea salt

grated zest of 1 orange

1 vanilla pod, split and seeds scraped, or 1 teaspoon vanilla extract

2 organic egg yolks

100 g (3½ oz) caster sugar

250 g (9 oz) tub ricotta, drained

1 teaspoon ground cinnamon

Start with the pastry. We need two discs and I find it easier to divide the ingredients in half and make two separate batches of dough so I don't overwork it. (You can of course make one large batch if you prefer – just handle it gently and divide it into two discs before resting.)

Use a fork to gently mix the egg yolks with the iced water in a small bowl. Keep in the fridge until ready to use.

Pulse the sugar, flour and salt in a food processor until combined, then add the butter and pulse until the mixture resembles breadcrumbs. With the motor running, quickly add the egg yolk and water mixture and blend until the dough comes together into a rough ball. Switch off as soon as this happens or you will overwork it.

Alternatively, if you don't have a food processor, put the sugar, flour and pinch of salt in a bowl and rub in the diced butter using your fingertips. Your hands should be cool and dry for this task. Once the butter is thoroughly rubbed in with no large lumps remaining, add the egg yolk mixture and combine with a fork to form a rough ball.

Tip the dough onto a lightly floured surface and gently bring it together, kneading once or twice with your hands. Shape the dough into a ball, then flatten it into a disc. Wrap it in cling film and rest in the fridge for 20 minutes. Repeat with the second batch of pastry.

To make the filling, combine the semolina, 200 ml (7 fl oz) water, a pinch of salt and half the orange zest in a small saucepan. Add the scraped vanilla seeds or extract. Cook over a medium heat for 3–5 minutes, stirring often with a wooden spoon. The semolina will start to thicken and become denser. It's ready when the texture is no longer grainy and you can draw a figure of eight when lifting the mixture with a spoon. Remove from the heat and set aside to cool for about 10 minutes.

Place the egg yolks and sugar in a large bowl and beat, using handheld electric beaters, for about 2 minutes until thick and pale. Whisk in the ricotta, cinnamon and remaining orange zest, beating for another minute or so until smooth and amalgamated. Whisk the semolina into the ricotta mixture, then set aside for at least 20 minutes to infuse and cool completely.

Remove the pastry from the fridge 10 minutes before assembling to make it a little easier to roll out.

Preheat the oven to 200°C (400°F) fan-forced. Grease a 25 cm (10 inch) tart tin and line the bottom with a disc of baking parchment.

Lightly flour the work surface and start rolling out one portion of the rested dough. Turn it 90 degrees after each roll to prevent it from sticking to the surface and ensure you are rolling it out evenly – ideally to a 5 mm (¼ inch) thickness.

Loosely fold the pastry disc around your rolling pin and transfer it to the tart tin, gently pressing it into place. Using a pastry brush, coat the bottom of the pastry case with a thin layer of beaten egg, then trim off any excess pastry and prick the base all over with a fork. Put the tin in the freezer for at least 10 minutes (or the fridge for 30 minutes) until the pastry is firm to the touch – this will stop it shrinking in the oven.

Meanwhile, roll out the second disc of pastry to a 5 mm (¼ inch) thickness and cut a circle slightly larger than the circumference of the tart tin, so that it will sit comfortably on top of the filling.

Retrieve the tart tin from the freezer or fridge and spoon in the ricotta filling, smoothing it out evenly. Carefully place the second pastry disc on top and pinch the pastry edges together to seal in the filling. If necessary, cut away any remaining excess pastry.

Brush the top with beaten egg, and make four leaf-shaped cuts with a sharp knife (in a loose cross shape) or simply cut four slits to allow the steam to escape. Put the pie in the oven and bake for 30 minutes or until the top is crisp and golden.

Meanwhile, peel the oranges, making sure you remove all the pith, then slice into 5 mm (¼ inch) thick discs. Place in a bowl until you are ready to serve.

Remove the pie from the oven and leave to cool for 10 minutes. Dust with icing sugar, then cut into slices and serve warm with a few slices of blood orange. This is also delicious for breakfast served at room temperature.

PALERMO AND NORTHERN SICILY

 The first time I visited Sicily was on the night boat from Naples. What a glamorous scene, you might think, but the reality was a bit less so. I was seven and it was mid-summer. My parents had forgotten to plan ahead which meant there were no cabins or seats left, so we all had to sleep on the floor by the bar. Soon after disembarking at Palermo, I remember my father stopping at a red light. A minute later a man on a moped crashed into the back of our stationary car and lay writhing on the ground, as twenty of his friends appeared out of nowhere to claim we had caused him a life-changing injury. It was, of course, a well-known scam and we escaped unscathed, but it taught me that in Sicily you must always be slightly on your guard.

That was twenty-five years ago, and in the many times I have returned to Sicily I have always felt a tingling excitement at the beauty, chaos and danger of this island, though nowadays they have cracked down on crime to attract more tourism. Today it is one of the twenty regions of Italy, but over the last few thousand years it has been occupied by everyone from the Greeks to the Moors to the Arabs and Turks and Spanish, their influences all felt in the temples and dialects they left behind. And, of course, the food. A perfect emblem of this is caponata, a typical sweet and sour dish of stewed aubergines and tomatoes which seems to combine all these disparate Mediterranean influences from over millennia into a single delicious pot. When you arrive in Sicily, but particularly Palermo, you feel far away from Europe, the hot fragrant air, and rows of palm trees giving the sense of being much closer to Africa than the northern parts of Italy or Europe.

The Sicilian approach to eating could be described as maximalist and is certainly not for anyone on a diet. If they can fry it or add sugar and cream, they will. Take breakfast for example. In Italy you might have a little plain croissant with your coffee. In Sicily they guzzle cornettos stuffed with cream or brioche buns filled with ice-cream or iced round cakes with a glacé cherry on top, said to resemble the breast of Catania's patron saint – Sant'Agata. Or perhaps all three, washed down with a coffee quite possibly covered in cream, and perhaps a little Marsala to finish off. Lunch might consist of deep-fried arancino (fist-sized balls of rice usually filled with meat ragu and peas) or the ultimate carb for carb lunch: panino di panelle, a sandwich stuffed with deep-fried chickpea flour fritters. The Sicilian enthusiasm for food is unsurprising given the bounty of the island grown from the mineral-rich volcanic soil from Mount Etna, the highest and most active volcano in Europe. Even the air smells wonderful in Sicily if you go at the right time of year – head there in May and you will be assaulted by the fragrance of zagara (orange blossom), which blooms extravagantly with pretty white flowers all over the island. The natural beauty of Sicily has inspired many a poet and has infused even the naming of some of their greedier dishes – in Palermo a deep-fried veal escalope, known everywhere else in Italy as a Milanese, is here known as Orecchio di elefante or an elephant's ear.

Sicily's two main cities of Palermo and Catania rival each other in everything, from their crumbling baroque palaces to their gastronomy. Even their respective arancini, both identical in flavour, differ in shape; those from Palermo are perfect spheres, whereas those from Catania have a lightly conical shape. Palermitani refer to theirs as an 'arancinA', whereas in Catania they are known as 'arancinO': apparently these are very important distinctions. Both also have exceptionally good markets, that of Palermo being in the old walls, around the corner from the city's gracious Norman duomo (cathedral). Catania's fish market, also by their duomo, boasts an array of every underwater creature you can imagine (including the odd shark), all gleaming from market stalls while locals shout about the quality and the price.

I love both cities, though some of my most treasured memories of Sicily took place in Catania, at the festival of Sant'Agata. Celebrated every year in early February in the shadow of Mount Etna, Sant'Agata is the largest Catholic festival in the world outside of Brazil, and local Catanesi wait all year for Saint Agata's remains to be taken from the city cathedral and carried around the city on ropes, supported by thousands of pilgrims all praying to her for various favours, help or protection. I saw one teenager carrying an enormous candle on her shoulder and chanting 'Siamo devoti tutti' (We are all devoted, long live Sant'Agata). When I asked her what she was praying for, she replied, 'I'm asking the saint to get my father out of jail early.' My friend Emily and I were late coming from the airport and the whole motorway simply shut down as everyone got out of their cars to scream and cheer and honk their horns as the night sky filled with fireworks and Sant'Agata's desiccated remains were paraded through the streets of Catania until dawn.

City life in Sicily is noisy and intense, it's not long before I find myself wanting to get away to the tranquillity of the countryside and coast. A favourite beach lies just a short drive out of Palermo, at Mondello bay, a perfect semi-circle of white sand and Caribbean blue water, where local families set up for the day. It is a very bucket-and-spade sort of place, with thousands of sun beds neatly lined up along the sand ready to be rented by the day or for the summer season by devoted Sicilian sun worshippers, or by anyone who simply needs an escape from the sweltering city. Children meander across the water on pedal boats, there are teenagers wind surfing and, my favourite, locals touting delicious tidbits up and down the beach for lunch. The self-professed 'Re del Mais' (King of Corn) sells deliciously steamed batons of salted and buttered corn on the cob – nothing tastes so good on a sunbed with a cold beer out of another vendor's ice box. For even quieter beaches, though, one must head east.

Sicily's northern shore abuts the Tyrrhenian Sea and is one of the most perfect 320 kilometre (200 mile) stretches of coastline anywhere in the world. A railway runs its entire length, from which you can watch Sicilian beach life roll by, played out on sandy beaches interrupted by the odd rocky outcrop and lovely baroque town. The train runs from Milazzo and Messina in the east to Palermo in the west. Incredibly, if travel from mainland Italy, your train will roll onto a ferry at Reggio Calabria and carry on the journey with you. (It's one of the few trains in the world that boards a ferry). Just hope that you don't come across Scylla, a once-beautiful nymph of whom Circe was jealous and so turned into a sea monster. Scylla was doomed to lurk in the narrow stretch of waters between Italy and Sicily, ready to eat any passing sailors. In *The Aeneid*, Virgil associates the narrow strip of water in which Scylla dwells opposite another monster, Charybdis, as the Strait of Messina. Being just an arrow's throw away from one another, the proximity of the two monsters meant that ships had to choose whether to be eaten by Scylla or drowned by Charybdis's whirlpool. The Calabrian seaside town of Scilla takes its name from the sea monster who lurked in its nearby waters. Only Odysseus was spared the fate that this duo of monsters had in store, successfully navigating the strait with the help of Circe who instructed him to 'hug Scylla's crag', rather than have his whole ship sunk in Charybdis's whirling water. The crag is purported to be the rocky headland known to the Greeks as Shyllaeum, the promontory on which the modern town of Scilla is built. Thankfully, as one chugs across this three-kilometre stretch of water, where the Tyrrhenian Sea gives way to the Ionian, sitting in one's train carriage on a ship, there is no sign of Scylla or Charybdis – only the alluring expanse of wine-dark sea.

Torta di fichi, noci e vin santo

FIG, WALNUT AND SWEET WINE CAKE

This cake is inspired by simple Tuscan baking, which is not overly sweet or elaborate. Its other inspiration is the island of Giglio, where figs grow in abundance, so naturally locals make many delicious fig desserts and sweets. The cake uses no butter in the batter, instead opting for Tuscan olive oil and sweet vin santo wine. If you can't find vin santo, you could use Marsala or, if really pushed, an equal mix of white wine and fortified pudding wine.

PREPARATION:– 20 minutes, plus cooling time
COOKING:– 1 hour

SERVES 8

butter, to grease the tin

2 organic eggs

220 g (8 oz) caster sugar

grated zest of 2 lemons

150 ml (5 fl oz) olive oil

100 ml (3½ fl oz) vin santo or other sweet wine

200 g (7 oz) '00' flour

1½ teaspoons baking powder

pinch of sea salt

100 g (3½ oz) walnuts, roughly chopped

4 ripe figs, sliced into thin discs

250 g (9 oz) creme fraiche

GLAZE

65 g (2¼ oz) runny honey

a few thyme sprigs, leaves picked

2 tablespoons vin santo

grated zest of 1 lemon

Preheat the oven to 180°C (350°F) fan-forced. Butter a round 24 cm (9½ inch) cake tin and line the base with baking parchment.

Put the eggs, sugar and lemon zest in a large bowl and beat with handheld electric beaters for 3–5 minutes until the mixture is very thick and pale. Combine the olive oil and vin santo in a measuring cup or jug, then gradually add to the egg mixture, beating to make sure each batch is incorporated before adding more.

Mix together the flour, baking powder and salt. Using a hand whisk, mix the dry ingredients into the wet ingredients to form a smooth batter. Stir in the chopped walnuts with a wooden spoon or spatula.

Pour the batter into the prepared tin and smooth the surface, creating a slight dip in the middle to prevent the centre from doming too much. Arrange the fig slices in a neat single layer on top, then place in the oven and bake for 40 minutes. Cover the top with foil, then bake for a further 10–15 minutes until golden brown and a cake tester inserted in the centre comes out clean.

Meanwhile, to make the glaze, put all the ingredients in a small saucepan over a medium heat. When the honey has liquified, leave the mixture to warm through and bubble for a couple of minutes. Remove from the heat and set aside to infuse until the cake is ready.

Leave the cake to cool in the tin for 30–45 minutes, then lightly prick the top around the figs and pour or brush over the glaze. (If it has become too solid to pour, gently warm it up again for a minute or two in the pan.) Remove the cake from the tin and transfer to a serving plate or cake stand.

Wait for the cake to cool completely, then serve in slices with a dollop of creme fraiche. Store in an airtight container for 3 days.

Torta caprese al limone con ganache al cioccolato

FLOURLESS LEMON AND ALMOND CAKE WITH CHOCOLATE GANACHE

This is a lemon version of the famous chocolate almond tort from the island of Capri. I love its nutty citrusy notes, particularly when paired with the smooth, velvety chocolate ganache. Whenever I see a lemon caprese on a restaurant menu I will order it, but am often downcast if the cake isn't lemony enough, which is partly why I started making it for myself at home and why this recipe calls for the zest of five lemons. It also just happens to be gluten-free.

PREPARATION:– 25 minutes, plus cooling time
COOKING:– 45 minutes

SERVES 8

butter, to grease the tin

100 g (3½ oz) blanched hazelnuts

75 g (2¾ oz) white chocolate, broken into pieces

25 g (1 oz) cornflour

1 teaspoon baking powder

pinch of sea salt

200 g (7 oz) caster sugar, plus 1 tablespoon, extra

200 g (7 oz) ground almonds

4 organic eggs, separated

grated zest of 5 lemons

juice of ½ lemon

90 g (3 oz) unsalted butter, melted

GANACHE

100 g (3½ oz) dark chocolate, broken into small pieces

150 ml (5 fl oz) double cream

1 tablespoon caster sugar

Preheat the oven to 180°C (350°F) fan-forced. Butter a round 20 cm (8 inch) cake tin and line the base with baking parchment.

In a food processor blitz the hazelnuts, white chocolate, cornflour, baking powder, salt and 1 tablespoon of caster sugar until roughly ground. Tip into a bowl, mix in the ground almonds and set aside.

Using handheld electric beaters, whisk the egg yolks, lemon zest and remaining sugar until thick and pale. Mix in the lemon juice and ground almond mixture. Pour over the melted butter to help the mixture come together more easily.

Whisk the egg whites until medium stiff peaks form, adding the extra tablespoon of sugar halfway through. Using a clean metal spoon, gently fold the egg whites into the almond mixture, bit by bit.

Pour the batter into the prepared tin and bake for 40 minutes or until a cake tester inserted in the centre comes out clean(ish). If it comes out covered in batter, bake for another 5 minutes and test again. Remove from the oven and leave to cool in the tin for 45–60 minutes before turning out onto a serving plate.

About 15 minutes before you turn out the cake, make the chocolate ganache. Place the chocolate in a large heatproof bowl. In a small saucepan, gently heat the cream and sugar, stirring until the sugar has dissolved. Bring to a simmer, then immediately remove from the heat. You don't want the cream to boil or it will split the ganache.

Pour the hot cream over the chocolate in the bowl and leave to sit for 2 minutes, then whisk thoroughly until thick and glossy. Let the ganache cool for 10 minutes – it should be a loose but spoonable consistency that won't run down the side of the cake.

Gradually spoon the ganache into the centre of the cake and smooth it out to the side using a spatula or the back of a spoon. Cut into slices and serve. The cake will keep in an airtight container for up to 3 days.

Delizia al limone

AMALFI LEMON CREAM CAKE

This cake is inspired by the delizie al limone served at the glorious bar-cum-bakery Pasticceria Panza in Amalfi, an old-fashioned place with mirrored walls, art deco signs and waiters in white gloves. It sits next to Amalfi's beautiful mosaic-domed cathedral in the main square, and is the perfect place for an aperitivo. But no matter what the hour, even if it's cocktail o'clock, I always have one of their signature lemon desserts. These come as individual domes: the outer layer is bright white lemony custard, while inside, held together by yet more lemon custard, are two airy layers of pan di spagna – a sponge made with no raising agent aside from air whose name presumably originated when Amalfi and the Kingdom of Naples were under Spanish rule.

I tried to recreate them at home and quickly concluded that making individual portions was best left to the master bakers, so instead I've made one large version as a cake. The result is rather like a very light but intensely creamy and lemony Victoria sponge. The original version covers the cake with custard mixed with lemon curd, but you can achieve the same indulgent citrusy feel by mixing lemon curd with whipped cream, cutting out the step of making the custard. It's still a bit of a marathon, but it's worth it and actually becomes more delicious the day after you've made it.

PREPARATION:– 40 minutes, plus cooling time
COOKING:– 25 minutes

Continues overleaf →

SERVES 8

300 ml (10 fl oz) double cream

grated lemon zest or edible flowers, to decorate (optional)

200 g (7 oz) strawberries, hulled and cut into quarters (optional)

SPONGE

butter, to grease the tins

4 organic eggs

120 g (4½ oz) caster sugar

grated zest of 2 lemons

120 g (4½ oz) '00' or plain flour

50 ml (1¾ fl oz) olive oil

LEMON CURD

2 organic eggs

3 organic egg yolks

120 g (4½ oz) caster sugar

grated zest of 3 lemons

juice of 2 lemons

100 g (3½ oz) unsalted butter, softened

LEMON SYRUP

80 g (2¾ oz) icing sugar

grated zest and juice of 1 lemon

To make the sponge cakes, preheat the oven to 180°C (350°F) fan-forced. Butter two 20 cm (8 inch) round cake tins and line the bases with baking parchment.

Crack the eggs into a large metal bowl, add the sugar and lemon zest and whisk with handheld electric beaters for 10–15 minutes (or, even better, use a stand mixer). This may sound like a long time, but remember there is no raising agent so the batter needs to be thoroughly whisked to ensure enough air is incorporated. It's ready when you can draw a figure of eight when lifting the mixture with a spoon and it sits on the surface for a few seconds; if it immediately sinks back into the batter, carry on whisking.

Sift in about a third of the flour and, using a clean metal spoon or spatula, very gently fold it into the egg mixture, being careful not to knock out any air. Fold in the rest of the flour, a third at a time, along with the olive oil. Pour the batter into the prepared tins and bake for 15 minutes or until a cake tester inserted in the centre comes out clean.

Don't remove the cakes from the oven just yet; instead, switch off the heat, prop the oven door slightly ajar with a wooden spoon and leave for 30 minutes so they cool gently. It's important to take this precaution as sharp changes in temperature may cause them to collapse.

Remove the cooled cakes from the oven and set aside to cool completely in the tins. At this point, the cakes will keep in a sealed container for up to 3 days.

Meanwhile, to make the lemon curd, combine the eggs, egg yolks, sugar, lemon zest and lemon juice in a small saucepan over a low heat. Use a whisk to stir and break up the eggs. Once the sugar has dissolved, increase the heat to medium and add half the butter; stir it in until melted, then repeat with the remaining butter. Stir constantly over the heat for about 5 minutes until the curd has thickened, then transfer the pan to a cool surface and keep mixing for a few more minutes. Set aside to cool completely. The curd will keep in a clean airtight container in the fridge for up to 3 days if you want to make it ahead of time.

For the lemon syrup, whisk together all the ingredients in a bowl until you have a thick sticky sauce.

When the cakes are completely cold you can start assembling your masterpiece. Prick one of the cakes all over with a skewer or fork, being careful not to go all the way to the bottom. Brush the top of the cake liberally with lemon syrup. Invert the other cake onto a serving plate or cake stand and prick it all over, being careful not to go all the way through. Brush liberally with lemon syrup.

Whip the cream to velvety soft peaks, about 2–3 minutes.

Pour half the lemon curd onto the cake sitting on the serving plate, smoothing it out evenly with the back of a spoon. Remove the other cake from its tin and top with a third of the whipped cream, smoothing it out to the edge. Carefully invert the cake onto the other one so the lemon curd and whipped cream layers are sandwiched together.

Add the rest of the lemon curd to the whipped cream to make a loose, thick lemony cream. Use the beaters to whisk for another minute or so to bring them together. Pour this over the top of the cake, using the back of a spoon or knife to smooth the surface, pushing some cream over the sides.

Cover the cake with a large upturned bowl and put it in the fridge for at least 2 hours before serving, or even better, let it chill overnight.

Remove the cake from the fridge about 20 minutes before serving. Decorate with lemon zest or edible flowers and serve with quartered strawberries, if you like.

PAVLOVA WITH PASSION FRUIT CURD

I was never a great one for making meringues until I started making custards and found I had mountains of egg whites left over. I turned to the queen of pavlovas, Skye McAlpine, who has a fabulous berry pavlova recipe in her beautiful book, *A Table for Friends*. It quickly became my go-to recipe when cooking for large groups. One day, I was cooking on one of the residential painting courses we host at the Arniano Painting School and a friend came to visit. He'd just been to Calabria and brought with him a bag of passion fruit that had grown in his host's garden. I was thrilled as I had no idea they grew on the southern stretch of the Tyrrhenian coast or, in fact, in Italy at all. I really wanted to do them justice and finally settled on a curd to drizzle over crispy meringues sandwiched together with whipped cream. It was a hit and is now a firm favourite with our painters. I often decorate it with a few sprigs of olive tree tucked in around the base of the meringue, but you could also use bay leaves or cow parsley, or sprinkle some blueberries over the top.

PREPARATION:– 35 minutes, plus cooling time
COOKING:– 1 hour 15 minutes

Continues overleaf →

SERVES 8–10

600 ml (20½ fl oz) double cream

MERINGUES

50 ml (1¾ fl oz) sunflower oil

2 teaspoons white wine vinegar

8 organic egg whites

400 g (14 oz) caster sugar

3 teaspoons cornflour

PASSION FRUIT CURD

10 passion fruit

100 g (3½ oz) caster sugar

2 organic eggs

3 organic egg yolks

100 g (3½ oz) unsalted butter, softened

To make the meringues, preheat the oven to 130°C (250°F) fan-forced. Line three baking sheets or wide roasting tins with baking parchment. Draw a circle on each piece of paper using a 24 cm (9½ inch) cake tin as a guide. Lightly brush the circles with sunflower oil to stop the meringues sticking.

Using 1 teaspoon of white wine vinegar and paper towel, scrupulously clean a large mixing bowl to beat your egg whites in – ideally the bowl of a stand mixer or any bowl large enough to accommodate handheld beaters. I often pass the vinegary paper over the beaters as well to ensure they are clean and free of fat.

Beat the egg whites until they begin to look frothy. Add a tablespoon of sugar and carry on whisking until the sugar has dissolved. With the whisk still running, gradually add the rest of the sugar, 1 tablespoon at a time. Once it has all been incorporated and the meringue is looking glossy, whisk in the cornflour and remaining vinegar.

Spoon the meringue equally into the circles on the lined trays, spreading it out with the back of the spoon to make three neat discs. Bake for 1 hour, then switch off the heat and leave the meringues to cool completely in the oven for another hour – this will ensure they are sturdy enough to assemble into the tower of cream and curd.

Meanwhile, prepare the curd. Cut each passion fruit in half and scoop the pulp into a bowl. Transfer the pulp to a medium saucepan, add the sugar, eggs and egg yolks and stir thoroughly to break up the eggs and encourage the sugar to dissolve. Set the pan over a medium heat. Add a third of the butter and keep stirring for a minute or so – the mixture should thicken and begin to coat the back of the spoon. Add the remaining butter bit by bit, stirring all the while for 5–7 minutes until the mixture becomes very thick. You should now have a lovely thick, orange curd dotted with black passion fruit seeds. Place the pan on a cool, heatproof surface and keep stirring for another 5 minutes to cool the curd.

If you are about to assemble the pavlova, you can leave the curd in the pan and use it directly from there. If you are making the curd ahead of time, store it in a clean airtight container in the fridge for up to 3 days, or in a sterilised jar (see page 232) for up to 1 week. Remove from the fridge an hour before assembling the pavlova so it comes to room temperature.

In a stand mixer or clean mixing bowl whip the double cream to velvety soft peaks. This should take about 3 minutes – be careful not to overwhisk or it will be a bit grainy.

Place the sturdiest meringue disc on a serving plate or cake stand. Spoon over a third of the whipped cream, smoothing it out to the edge with the back of a spoon. Using a tablespoon, randomly dollop over a third of the passion fruit curd, making sure that some spills over the side. Add the second meringue disc and repeat with another layer of cream and curd. Place the third meringue disc on top and finish with the last of the cream and curd.

Serve within a few hours. Any leftovers can be kept in an airtight container in the fridge and will be delicious the next day as a sort of exotic Eton Mess.

Limoncello

ONE-WEEK LIMONCELLO

I had never been a fan of limoncello until I tried it on the Amalfi Coast. To me the flavour was always too synthetic, but when I tasted homemade limoncello made from Amalfi lemons my mind changed. The cold citrus hit in a good-quality alcohol has a flavour of its own and is easy to recreate. I now always have a bottle in the freezer, ready to serve in a limoncello spritz (page 45), a boozy lemon tiramisu (page 205), poured over lemon granita (page 200) or simply to enjoy as a digestif. You can buy wonderful lemons now in most places but avoid using the small waxed supermarket ones. While I was embarking on my love affair with homemade limoncello I had a conversation with a young woman from Norfolk whose mother is from Campania. Her mother makes limoncello as well as cremino di limone – the lemon equivalent of a Baileys, very creamy, alcoholic and indulgent. I was fascinated to hear that, as you need pure ethanol (which is banned in the UK), her mother would smuggle bottles in her children's suitcases when returning from visiting family. I applaud her determination but recommend sticking to this recipe.

PREPARATION:– 15 minutes, plus sterilising and standing time
COOKING:– 5 minutes

**MAKES 1.5 LITRES
(51 FL OZ)**

7 unwaxed lemons (if you can find the large kind with leaves from Amalfi, all the better)

1 x 700 ml (23½ fl oz) bottle good-quality vodka

300 g (10½ oz) caster sugar

Before you start you'll need to sterilise a 1.5 litre (51 fl oz) Kilner jar (or two 1 litre/ 34 fl oz bottles). Preheat the oven to 110°C (225°F) fan-forced.

Wash the jar in hot soapy water and rinse well. Remove the rubber ring and boil in a small saucepan of water for 5 minutes, then drain and leave to dry in a colander while you sterilise the jar. Place the open jar on a baking tray in the oven for about 12 minutes to dry out. Switch off the heat and open the oven door slightly to allow the glass to cool completely – this should take 15–20 minutes.

Rinse and thoroughly dry the lemons. Using a vegetable peeler, carefully remove the lemon peel in long strips, being careful not include too much of the bitter white pith – you only want the rind.

Place the strips in the cooled sterilised jar and pour over the vodka. Close the lid and store in a cool, dark place for 7 days, allowing the lemon to infuse into the alcohol. During this time the vodka will take on a glorious sunshine yellow colour.

After 7 days, combine the sugar and 700 ml (23½ fl oz) water in a saucepan over a medium heat, stirring a little to encourage the sugar to dissolve. Bring the water to the boil, then immediately switch off the heat and set the syrup aside to cool completely.

Add the cooled syrup to the lemony vodka and stir well. If you have used a jar you may want to decant it into bottles (use a funnel if you prefer it without lemon peel). Pour the limoncello into the two sterilised bottles (one will be full and the other half full). Label and store in the freezer for whenever the need strikes.

ACKNOWLEDGEMENTS

Raising a baby is said to take a village, and I would say this also applies to producing a cookbook. Having now done both at the same time, I have more of a sprawling metropolis of people to thank. First my husband, Matthew, my biggest cheerleader, who came on every research trip (a great hardship), read countless drafts of the manuscript and took time off work to look after our son while I wrote it. To Mama, who always supports me in a myriad of ways, even more so since I became a parent, as do my wonderful in-laws, Nick and Olwen Bell.

Thank you to my publisher, Kirsten Abbott, for believing in my ambitious but vague idea and trusting that it would come together to create this beautiful book. Your faith in me is one of the things I am most grateful for in my professional life. To my fantastic agent, Laurie Robertson, your support and encouragement know no bounds, as I am reminded every time you are there for me on a dawn Zoom to Australia. To Ashlea O'Neill, for her gorgeous, original designs and layouts. To everyone at Thames & Hudson who contributed to the creation of *Italian Coastal*: Shannon Grey, Anna Carlsson and Caitlin O'Reardon. To my editor, Rachel Carter, who martialled my thoughts and brought the text together so beautifully. A huge thank you to my oldest friend, Savannah Alvarez, for all the research, support and for being there for me and Milo.

The recipes would not sing without their accompanying photographs, for which I am so grateful to Saghar Setareh. Thank you for bringing your wonderful eye to the project and for bringing my recipes to life through your images. To our producer and food stylist, Alice Adams, thank you for all your support and for ensuring the shoots ran smoothly and we got the most fabulous shots possible, including some impressive acrobatics to keep a tile background steady. To all the team at Latteria Studio in Rome: Benedetta Canale, Rossella Venezia and Niamh Richardson. To everyone at Arniano for making the shoot there possible: Rossana Lippi, Marcella Testai, Grazia Flores, Said El Arfaoui and Jessica Ramirez. Thank you to Tara Guinness of Tara Cookery, who made sure that all the recipes work in a non-Italian kitchen and with non-Italian produce. To Georgina Hayden for her brilliant advice on recipe testing with a newborn. To my mother-in-law and formidable cook, Andrea Lechner, thank you for your tests and feedback on the entire 'From the Sea' chapter and to Colin for his photos of the dishes.

The recipes in this book are a collection of things that I have loved eating on my travels along Italy's Tyrrhenian coast and islands, and I want to thank all the people who either shared a recipe with me or cooked something that inspired me when I got home: Anita and the whole team at the Principe di Salina, Samuele e Federica, Maurizia from Sapori Eoliani and Viviana from Garavicchio. To Flaminia Perez from La Guardia Hotel on Giglio, everyone from Carmen Bay in Maremma, Alessandro Grassi for sending me to Capofaro, Fabio and Barbara of Chez Barone Cooking School, Antonella Gorga from Il Cannito in Cilento, everyone at Tenuta Vannulo, Lisa Corti's Emporium in Milan, Margherita e Antonia from Lo Scoglio, Luca del Bono, Giuseppe Tasca, Alek and Zsofia, Sebastian and the countless restaurants that got me thinking. Thank you as well to all the friends and family who supported me in ways large and small: Claudia Guinness, Liberty Nimmo, Beata Heuman, John Finlay, Ali and Jack Coleman, Sue Townsend, Marella Caracciolo Chia, Natalie Rucellai, Ben and Juliette Ashworth, Georgina Smith, Isabella Worsley, Grace Pilkington, David Macmillan, William Roper-Curzon, Panos Varoutsos, Luke Edward Hall and Duncan Campbell, Barù della Gherardesca, Eleanor Daunt, Emily FitzRoy and Fiona Corsini. And finally, to Robyn Lea, without whom I might not be writing cookbooks. You are such an inspiration, and the embodiment of a successful woman lifting up another woman who needed a little nudge in the right direction.

INDEX

AMBER GUINNESS

Amber Guinness is an English cook and food writer living in Florence. She was born in London but raised at Arniano, the Tuscan farmhouse her parents restored near Siena. She studied history and Italian literature at the University of Edinburgh, working as a cook in both London and Italy in her spare time. Amber's first book, *A House Party in Tuscany*, featured recipes and stories from her internationally acclaimed residential painting school at Arniano. *Italian Coastal* is her second book. Amber is married with a son.

First published in Australia in 2024
by Thames & Hudson Australia Pty Ltd
11 Central Boulevard, Portside Business Park
Port Melbourne, Victoria 3207
ABN: 72 004 751 964

First published in the United Kingdom in 2024
by Thames & Hudson Ltd
181a High Holborn
London WC1V 7QX

First published in the United States of America in 2024
by Thames & Hudson Inc.
500 Fifth Avenue
New York, New York 10110

Italian Coastal © Thames & Hudson Australia 2024

Text © Amber Guinness
Images © Saghar Setareh
© Amber Guinness (pp. 8, 10, 12, 14, 15, 18, 22, 25, 40, 50, 53, 66, 67, 73, 74, 77, 78, 90, 91, 98, 101, 102, 117, 118, 119, 121, 130, 134, 137, 143, 149, 150, 151, 160, 178, 182, 195, 196, 197, 199, 211, 218, 221, 234)

27 26 25 24   5 4 3 2 1

The moral right of the author has been asserted.

Thames & Hudson Australia wishes to acknowledge that Aboriginal and Torres Strait Islander people are the first storytellers of this nation and the Traditional Custodians of the land on which we live and work. We acknowledge their continuing culture and pay respect to Elders past and present.

ISBN 978-1-760-76365-7 (hardback)
ISBN 978-1-760-76433-3 (U.S. edition)
ISBN 978-1-760-76443-2 (ebook)

A catalogue record for this book is available from the National Library of Australia

British Library Cataloguing-in-Publication Data

A catalogue record for this book is available from the British Library

Library of Congress Control Number 2023948378

Every effort has been made to trace accurate ownership of copyrighted text and visual materials used in this book. Errors or omissions will be corrected in subsequent editions, provided notification is sent to the publisher.

Front cover design: Ashlea O'Neill | Salt Camp Studio
U.S. cover design: Salt Camp Studio
Design and illustration: Ashlea O'Neill | Salt Camp Studio
Printed and bound in China by C&C Offset Printing Co., Ltd

FSC® is dedicated to the promotion of responsible forest management worldwide. This book is made of material from FSC®-certified forests and other controlled sources.

MIX
Paper | Supporting
responsible forestry
FSC® C008047

Be the first to know about our new releases, exclusive content and author events by visiting
thamesandhudson.com.au
thamesandhudson.com
thamesandhudsonusa.com